AF587705

ISBN-nummer: 90-784-6401-1
EAN-code: 9 789078 464013
Wettelijk depotnummer: D/2006/Birgit van de Wijer, uitgever

April 2006

CHILD EXODUS
FROM TIBET

Birgit van de Wijer

This book is dedicated
to all the Tibetans who crossed my path and enriched my life
and
to those who did not survive their escape to freedom.

REFUGEE

When I was born
my mother said
you are a refugee.
Our tent on the roadside
smoked in the snow.

On your forehead
between your eyebrows
there is an **R** embossed
my teacher said.

I scratched and scrubbed,
on my forehead I found
a brash of red pain.

I have three tongues.
The one that sings
is my mother tongue.

The **R** on my forehead
between my English and Hindi
the Tibetan tongue reads:

RANGZEN

Freedom means Rangzen

Tenzin Tsundue, *Kora. Stories and Poems* (Dharamsala 2002), p. 18.

ACKNOWLEDGMENTS

My warmest thanks to my friends who understood what this book meant to me and supported me financially or morally from the very beginning, even before a publisher could be found: Anne, Gudula, Tine, Véronique, Catherine, the Kerckhofs family, Christel, and some friends who prefer to remain anonymous.

ཐུགས་རྗེ་ཆེ། (=Thujechhe, thank you) to Phuntsok Dhondup because our conversation about Tibet in 1998 changed my life course and also for your help with the translation during my interviews; ཐུགས་རྗེ་ཆེ། to Sangpo and Dawa for your friendship, hospitality and generosity. Room 504 in Norsang's guesthouse was a very inspiring place! ཐུགས་རྗེ་ཆེ། to Phurbu Dolma, my companion on my trip, for your translations from Nepali, Tibetan and Hindi, for being my 'memory', my best cook, my ever smiling best friend; ཐུགས་རྗེ་ཆེ། to Tenzin Yangkyi, Kyi-so, Tenzin Nangsen, Lama Jigme, and Tenzin Chompel, my other translators; ཐུགས་རྗེ་ཆེ། to the freelance reporter for the Tibetan Centre of Human Rights and Democracy (*TCHRD*) in Nepal, for your precious information; ཐུགས་རྗེ་ཆེ། to the rest of the Reception Centre Staff in Kathmandu and to the *THF* staff for your hospitality and effectiveness during my brief stay. ཐུགས་རྗེ་ཆེ། to Tenzin Tsundue for his kind permission to publish his 'Refugee' poem.

Many thanks to Kate (*ICT*) for your precious comments and help; to my friend Marc, my so-called layman in the field, for your astute remarks and multiple translations; to Paul for your excellent comments and additions; to Luc and Piet for your professional help in preparing the pictures; to all those who supported me in any way; and to Dmitri, for calling my book 'the last hope for humanity'.

Last but not least to my family: without your continuous support, advice and effective help I would never have managed to reach the finishing line. My greatest thanks to my mother and father for their guidance and wise advice.

Birgit
April 2006

TABLE OF CONTENTS

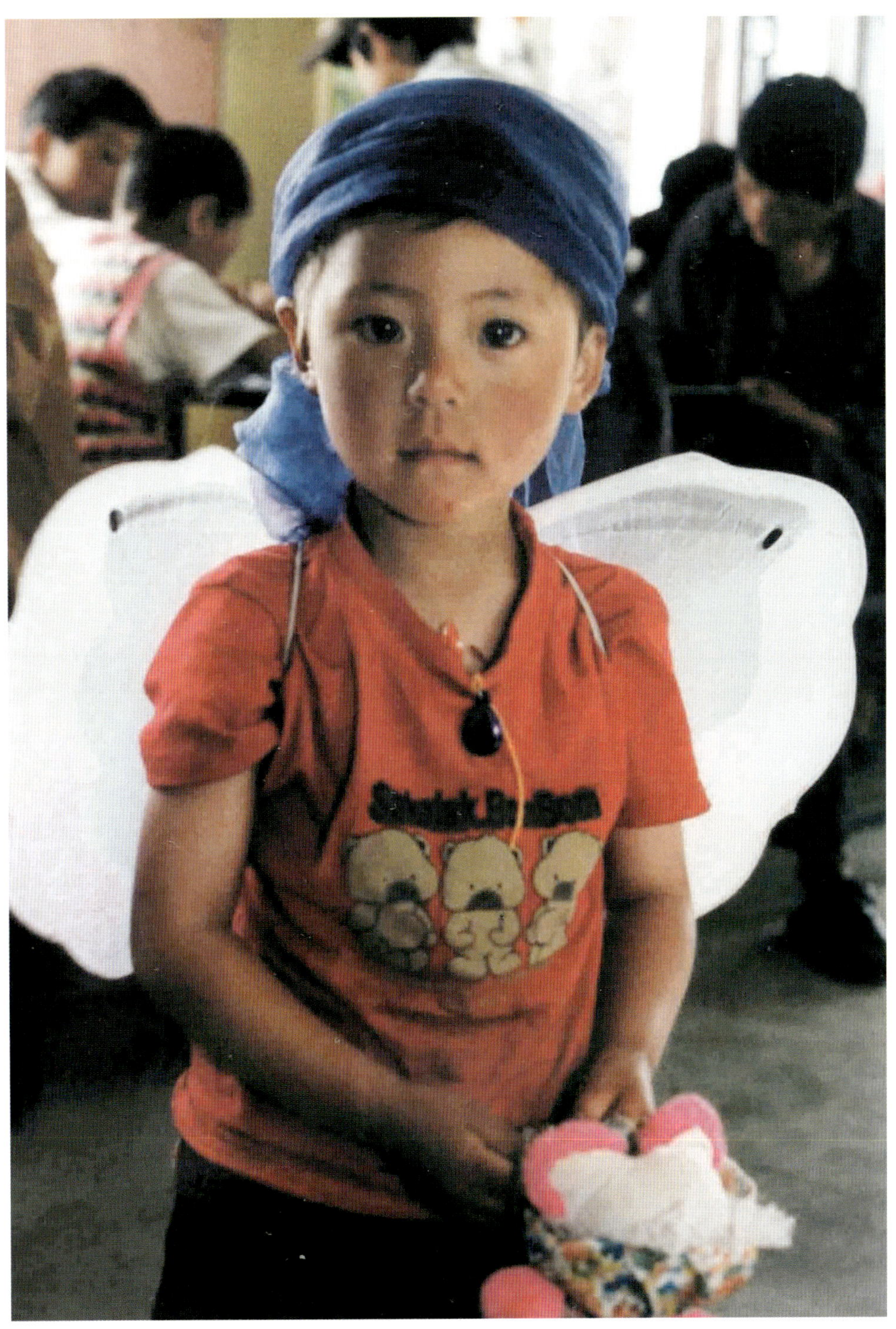

Girl in the Reception Centre in Kathmandu
March 2003

FOREWORD

Tibetan children fleeing their country across the Himalayas in search of education may seem a merely 'anecdotal' story.[1] However, the more I have been reading about the number of children each year, their reasons, the risks of their journeys, the more I felt the need to write this book.

It all started in March 2003 while I was researching an article about the *Tibetan Children Villages (TCV)* in India, a network of schools for children who escaped from Tibet. My friend Sangpo advised me to visit the *Tibetan Refugee Reception Centre (TRRC)* in Kathmandu (Nepal) since all children first transit there before leaving for India. I visited the centre and its classroom that was packed with children of all ages. Kyi-So, one of the female teachers, was dressing the youngest up as little fairies, while Tsering Yangchen was teaching the English alphabet to the older ones. For the first time I realized how numerous these child refugees were, and that some of them were very small. I wondered how they had managed to make a 1,000-km [2] journey and cross the Himalayas. Then I went to Dharamsala (India) where I met a young woman with her two month-old baby. She related her journey and the capture of her husband and her five year-old son by the Chinese. Images of this imprisoned boy kept haunting my mind, spurring me on to find out more about this subject.

In 2005 I decided to travel to Nepal and India for a longer period to interview the newly arrived children and to complete my research on the subject. For one month, from 15 November on, I visited the *TRRC* in Kathmandu and witnessed that the centre was overcrowded. Not only do most of the refugees risk the dangerous crossing at this time of the year, but the Nepalese government had stopped issuing exit permits to India. The total number of refugees exceeded 1,200,[3] in a centre built for 200: an inhuman situation.

Young people who lost their toes to frostbite, a young man and his pregnant wife locked up for 8 days in a room full of cow dung and forced to eat it due to lack of food, 18 youngsters kept in prison for 11 days, ... all of them shared their story with me.

It became hard to stay insensitive.

---

[1] This was the response of the Journalistic Fund Pascal Decroos (Belgium) to my request for financial support.
[2] The distance between Lhasa and Kathmandu is about 1,000 km.
[3] Number on 20 December 2005.

INTRODUCTION

'Tibetans who fled to India are not ordinary refugees. (...) Above all, they could bring with them the most important person in their society: the Dalai Lama.'[1]

After the escape of the *Dalai Lama* in 1959, thousands of Tibetans followed him into exile in India. Even now more than 2,000 Tibetans cross the Himalayas each year: monks, nuns, nomads, farmers, ex-prisoners and ... children. They all feel imprisoned in their own country and flee to a new life.

'In Tibet Chinese don't regard Tibetans as humans. Monks and nuns are forced to learn whatever the Chinese tell them, they are indoctrinated and often expelled from their monasteries. For farmers and nomads surviving becomes very difficult due to the high taxes on their cattle, their lands, their fences. They have no choice but to accept to shift to the city, in small rooms at a very high rate. Moreover, Chinese sometimes chase them away, so that they can extract precious minerals from their lands. Ex-political prisoners are constantly supervised after being released and opportunities to rebuild a new life are very rare.'[2]

Last but not least, thousands of children have no access to good education in their own language; due to the Chinese occupation this is no longer possible in Tibet.

How many children have already been sent to India for an education in schools under the authority of the *Dalai Lama*? Nobody knows the exact number, since hundreds or even thousands of them have not succeeded in reaching India.

Why do the parents not flee together with their children? Some of them do, but after delivering their child to school, they return home. Most of them are nomads: poor, uneducated people unable to find employment in India. Moreover, the same parents have to care for the older generation, their own parents. Family ties are strong in Tibet. Parents simply have no choice but to trust strangers to get their children 'to school'.

Most literature concerning the flight of these children is either romanticized or piled up on the dusty shelves of libraries that no one enters. This is not to detract from the excellent job done by the *International Campaign for Tibet (ICT) or the Tibet Justice Center (TJC)*, whose brochures are aimed at people already interested in the subject.

We want to reveal this problem to a larger public.

---

[1] Tanka B. SUBBA, *Flight and Adaptation. Tibetan Refugees in the Darjeeling-Sikkim Himalaya* (Dharamsala, 1990), p. 28.

[2] Interview with a freelance reporter for the Tibetan Centre for Human Rights and Democracy (TCHRD) in Nepal, November 2005. (See also in appendix 2).

HISTORICAL BACKGROUND[3]

Since early times the history of Tibet has seen successive periods of war and peace with its neighbours – Nepal, Mongolia and especially China – and alternating periods of dependency and autonomy. The Manchu rulers of China invaded in 1720 and established their overlordship of Tibet, but in the course of time this became largely nominal. It was violently reasserted by the imperial government in 1910, in reaction to British interference in Tibet, but when the Republic of China was proclaimed in 1911, Tibet proclaimed its own independence. The British Empire jealously watched over the independence of Tibet: not wanting it for themselves, they did not want to see Russia or China in control of India's mountainous northern frontier. At that time only 6,000,000 Tibetans lived in Tibet, a country with six times the surface area of France; China numbered 1,000,000,000 inhabitants and India 860,000,000. Small wonder that Tibet's neighbours looked at it with greedy eyes.

In 1947, when India became independent, the British stopped their interference in Tibet. In October 1949 the People's Republic of China was proclaimed and the People's Liberation Army (PLA) established Communist rule over Tibet east of the Yangzi River, which since 1933 had been under the occupation of the Chinese Nationalists.

On 5 October 1950, with the world's attention focused on Korea, the PLA crossed the Yangzi and captured Chamdo, the headquarters of the Governor of Eastern Tibet. It was an unprovoked invasion of independent Tibet. In November 1950, the Tibetan Government lodged a protest against Chinese aggression with the United Nations, but the General Committee indefinitely postponed placing the issue on the agenda of the General Assembly, and further appeals that the protest be addressed fell on deaf ears.

On 23 May 1951, a Tibetan delegation which had gone to Beijing to negotiate with the Chinese was forced to sign the so-called '17-point Agreement on Measures for the Peaceful Liberation of Tibet', an agreement that put an end to Tibet's independence with threats of more military action. The Chinese published the terms before they had been ratified by Lhasa, and then used this document to carry out their plans to turn Tibet into a colony of China, disregarding the strong resistance of the Tibetan people. What is more, in time they violated every article of this unequal 'treaty' which they had imposed on the Tibetans.

On 9 September 1951, thousands of Chinese troops marched into the capital, Lhasa. Although at first cautious and conciliatory in Tibet west of the Yangzi, the Chinese incorporated the eastern regions of Tibet into the bordering provinces of China. There,

[3] Information derived from Jonathan SPENCE, *In Search of Modern China* (2nd edition, New York and London, 1999); Dawa NORBU, *China's Tibet Policy* (Richmond, 2001); Melvyn C. GOLDSTEIN, with the help of Gelek Rimpoche, *A History of Modern Tibet, 1913-1951. The Demise of the Lamaist State* (Berkeley, Los Angeles and London, 1989); Tsering SHAKYA, *The Dragon in the Land of Snows. A History of Modern Tibet since 1947* (London, 1999); the broadcast 'Tibet, a chronicle of a tragedy', transmitted on Canvas (Belgian Television) on June 1, 2005; and 'Chronology of Contemporary Events.' An Information *Sheet of the Department of Information and International Relations of the Tibetan government-in-exile (DIIR).*

the occupation was marked by systematic destruction of monasteries, suppression of religion, denial of political freedom, widespread arrests and imprisonment, and the massacre of innocent men, women and children.

In 1954 the *Dalai Lama* was invited to Beijing and the Chinese informed him of their plans for the reform of Tibet.

In April 1956 China set up a Preparatory Committee for the Autonomous Region of Tibet (PCART) to replace the Tibetan government. During his trip to India in November for the celebration of Buddha's birthday, the *Dalai Lama* appealed to India for help against the Chinese invaders, but Prime Minister Nehru refused to intervene.

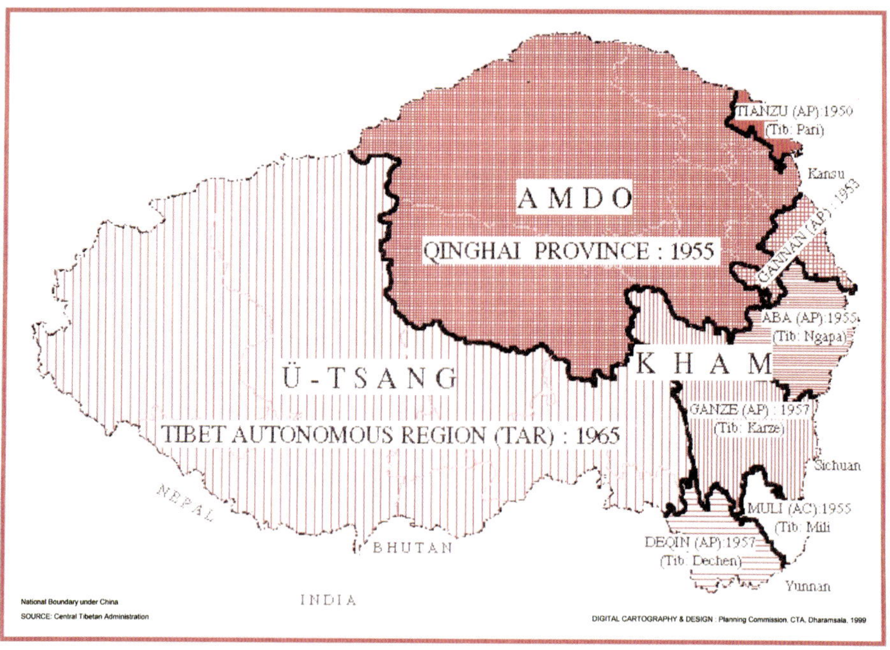

Tibet Autonomous Region (TAR).

On 10 March 1959, the nation-wide Tibetan resistance culminated in the Tibetan National Uprising against the Chinese. Thousands of men, women and children were massacred in the streets of Lhasa and many more imprisoned and deported. Monks and nuns were a prime target. Monasteries and temples were shelled. Martial law was proclaimed. Since it was the period of the Cold War and the Cuban crisis, the Chinese had free scope: in the whole country more than 100,000 people died from exhaustion, hunger, terror, rape. Monks were buried alive; children were forced to shoot their parents ...

Every year this date is remembered by Tibetans and their sympathizers all over the world.

Tibetan flags at the remembrance meeting held in Paris in March 2002 to commemorate the Lhasa uprising.

On 17 March 1959 the *Dalai Lama* left Lhasa and escaped from the pursuing Chinese to seek political asylum in India. He was followed into exile by an unprecedented exodus of 80,000 Tibetans.

A government-in-exile was formed and on 10 March 1963 the democratic constitution was proclaimed.

Towards the end of 1962 the 10th *Panchen Lama*, who still had influential friends in Beijing, openly criticized the disastrous effects of Communist policies. In August 1964, 10,000 Tibetan students demonstrated in Lhasa against Chinese policies. In September the *Panchen Lama* was purged, not to be seen in public again until March 1978.

Mao's Cultural Revolution (1966-1976) unleashed a further wave of death and destruction.

In July 1979 Deng Xiaoping announced a policy of liberalization leading to the release of thousands of Tibetan prisoners.

In June 1984 the Tibetan government-in-exile announced the death of 1.2 million Tibetans as a direct result of Chinese invasion and occupation.[4]

The *Dalai Lama* presented his 'Five Point Peace Plan' to the American Senate in September 1987. At the same time, in Lhasa, thousands of Tibetans walked around the Jokhang temple (main temple) while carrying the forbidden[5] *Tibetan flag*, claiming independence and demanding the withdrawal of Chinese troops. Similar protests took place six months and one year later before the eyes of tourists and foreign journalists. Again the Chinese answer was a bloody one: repression and martial law.

At the Third Tibet Work Forum in June 1994, China's top leadership, in the name of economic development, unleashed the most intensive repression of Tibetan religion and nationalism since the end of the Cultural Revolution.

In April 1996 the 'Strike Hard' Campaigns for patriotic re-education and spiritual civilization began. Aimed at coercing the Tibetans to renounce their faith in the *Dalai Lama,* monasteries and nunneries were especially targeted.

In June 2001 China's Fourth Work Forum on Tibet endorsed the repressive policies of the Third Forum (1994) and called for the acceleration of Tibet's integration into the economy and culture of China.

This policy of extermination, imposed over several decades, has in combination with the mass resettlement of Chinese Han in Tibet resulted in Tibetans being a minority in their own country.

Since a solution will not be found tomorrow, Tibetans continue to flee even today.

---

[4] In his book *Tibet, Tibet. A personal history of a lost land.* (New Delhi, 2003), pp. 288-294, Patrick FRENCH rejects the number of 1,200,000 that has been often cited as an uncontested fact even in independent publications. This number seems to rest on hearsay and not on any verifiable source and was given by the Tibetan government-in-exile in response to demands of foreign supporters of the Tibetan cause. A systematic overview of the numbers involved was needed to impress Western legislators. While outside researchers were never allowed access to the documentation on which it is based, P. French could do so. Although he quickly found that this number was exaggerated, he states that this in no way diminishes the immense suffering and persecution of the Tibetans under the Chinese. It is probable that as many as 500,000 died as a direct result of Chinese policy.

[5] In Tibet, the Tibetan flag is strictly forbidden by the Chinese, as are pictures and videos of H.H. the Dalai Lama. People cannot even have them at home and may end up in prison if they do.

CHAPTER 1

WHY DO CHILDREN FLEE?

'I never went to school.
I studied Tibetan language
on my own while I was looking
after the animals.'
(Anonymous refugee)

The main reason for Tibetan children to flee their country is that they seek an education that is no longer available in the *Tibet Autonomous Region*, or *TAR* (see the map in the previous chapter). Not only do most of the schools have Chinese as the language of instruction, but school fees are expensive, even more so for Tibetans. Furthermore, some parents do not want their children spoiled by the Chinese way of living. A few children even flee without the knowledge of their parents.

The reasons why parents send their children to India in massive numbers are all related to Chinese education policy in Tibet: marginalization of the Tibetan language, culture and religion, high school fees, lack of access, and poor quality of education. The statements in the book *State of Education in Tibet,* published by the Tibetan Centre of Human Rights and Democracy (*TCHRD*)[1] are confirmed by other Tibet support groups *(TJC, ICT, TIN)* and also by UN reporters, so-called Rapporteurs.

Although China ratified the *Convention on the Rights of the Child (CRC)* and several international conventions that include the basic right to education, there is a big gap between theory and practice, and a number of rights are clearly violated.

'Education of the child shall be directed to the development of respect for the child's parents, his/her own cultural identity, language and values, for the national values of the country in which the child is living.' (CRC art.29)

In practice, Tibetan students rarely receive any lessons on their culture or history. They are not allowed to honour any Tibetan holiday except Tibetan New Year, and they cannot wear Tibetan clothes at school.[2] The teaching of the Tibetan language is marginalized to the advantage of Chinese, despite the fact that it has been proven that students perform better when they receive instruction in their mother tongue.[3] In most rural areas Tibetan students still receive primary education in Tibetan, while students in urban areas have started receiving it in Chinese. Tibetan children only receive Chinese language courses in grades three and four. At the end of primary school, however, all of them have to perform an entrance test in Chinese since this is the language of instruction in all secondary schools. Many Tibetans from rural areas do not speak Chinese; failing their entrance exam means they cannot gain access to education beyond primary level and are unable to continue further studies. To undertake higher studies, as well as to enter the job market, knowledge of Chinese has become a must.[4]

'The Tibetan subject is not taught; it's seen as a less important subject, Chinese language is seen as important. If you have studied Chinese language, after you have

[1] *State of Education in Tibet. A Human Rights Perspective* (Dharamsala, 2004).

[2] International Committee of Lawyers for Tibet, *A Generation in Peril. The Lives of Tibetan Children under Chinese Rule: A Report* (Berkeley, Cal., 2001), p. 67.

[3] Mother Tongue as the Medium of Instruction in Schools in Tibetan Review, April 2004, p. 25.

[4] *State of Education in Tibet,* pp. 36-37, 45.

finished school, you will get a job easily. If you study Tibetan language, you won't. That's why so many children flee.'[5]

'Primary education shall be compulsory and available free to all.' (CRC art. 28)

Large numbers of children have no access to a school. The *TAR* is the most disadvantaged region of all China, with the highest illiteracy rate for Tibetans ages six and up, estimated at 49.1%, compared with the nation-wide average of 13.7%.[6] This was also proved by statements of children in the *Tibetan Refugee Reception Centre (TRRC)* in Kathmandu.[7] Most of them had never been to school.

'I was brought up by my eldest sister since our parents passed away when I was very small. I had never been to school since school fees were too expensive.' (aged 11)

'I came here with my four brothers. The youngest is only five years old. I had never been to school.' (aged 12)

'I am looking forward to going to school. In my village there was no school and no electricity either.' (aged 10)

In Tibet education is not only not for free; it is very expensive, even more for Tibetans than for the Chinese.

'I escaped because I want to study Tibetan and learn more about Tibet. In my town school fees were very high and my parents couldn't pay them.' (aged 12)

'I had been to school for three years in Lhasa, but my school was closed by the Chinese government. My parents couldn't afford to send me to another school.' (aged 8)

Many parents cannot afford the school fees, which sometimes come to as much as 300 *Yuan* per month,[8] twice the average monthly salary.[9] The cost of the fees depends on whether or not someone possesses a 'themto pass', a document that authorizes the person to live in that area. A 'themto pass' is required to send your children to school, to receive health care, to own a house. To acquire such a pass, bribes need to be paid to the officials.[10] Next to the fees for tuition, uniforms and books, Tibetan parents are compelled to pay 'miscellaneous' fees to the school authorities in order to supplement the low teachers' salaries, to cover the maintenance cost of the buildings.[11] In addition

[5] Interview with a freelance reporter for TCHRD in Nepal, November 2005.
[6] *Alternative Report for the Committee on the Rights of the Child. Violations of the Convention on the Rights of the Child in Tibetan Autonomous Areas of China* (ICT, 2005), p. 2.
[7] Statements copied from the notebook of Tsering Yangchen, one of the teachers in the *TRRC* in Kathmandu. When copying her record of these children's words they are identified only by their age, for example '(aged 11)'. My own informants are referred to in terms such as 'a 16 year-old girl'. This practice has been followed throughout.
[8] 100 *Yuan* is roughly equivalent to €10 or $12.
[9] *TJC Newsletter* (July 2005).
[10] *State of Education*, p. 43.
[11] *A Generation in Peril*, p. 49.

to this, Tibetan parents are often asked to buy supplies (for example 1 kg of butter, a leg of mutton, 2 kg of roasted barley flour, 1½ kg of rice and 2 kg of wheat).[12] In some cases, Tibetan children are even forced to perform labour and other tasks, such as cooking for the teacher, sweeping, or cleaning the latrines.[13]

'The Chinese government always lies. In advertising they say the school fees in Tibet are free, but actually they are not. At this moment in Tibet the students face problems to go higher in education since the school fees are very high. School fees are even higher when you go to a higher class. Most of the people in Tibet are very poor; families have many members, so it's very difficult to send all the children to school. Therefore, most of the Tibetan children in rural areas simply don't go, while children from the city, and of course the children of Chinese government officials, can get higher education. Even if a student from a very rich family is not good in education, they just buy the certificate. But a student from a poor family, even if he is good, he cannot afford school, so he cannot study. This is the big difference between Chinese and Tibetan students. So many parents, even when they are poor, they borrow money from their friends or from their family, like 3000 or 4000 Chinese *Yuan*, and they send their children to Nepal and then further to India for education. Even though parents are poor they try to give their children education.'[14]

In schools, several forms of discrimination are common. The Chinese pay much lower fees or even have free education, and they are not forced to bring all kind of items to school. Chinese pupils also have better classrooms than Tibetans, and they can use computers while the others cannot. Chinese students are even encouraged by their teachers to harass their Tibetan fellow-students.

Even if a Tibetan student passes his entrance exam, this does not mean he is accepted. It is bribes and the use of connections that decide whether a student is allowed to start secondary school.[15]

In some cases, brilliant Tibetan students are removed from their communities and sent to special boarding schools in Beijing or Chengdu. This increases the chances of dislocation and assimilation for the individuals, while simultaneously robbing local Tibetan communities of their brightest young people.[16]

'A child belonging to a minority shall not be denied the right to enjoy his own culture, to practice his own religion, or to use his own language.' (CRC art.30)

The greatest form of discrimination is ethnic: Tibetans are forced to celebrate Chinese holidays, learn about Chinese culture in the Chinese language, and learn the Chinese version of their own history. Most Tibetans educated through the medium of Chinese lose their ability to read and write Tibetan.[17] In 1988 Tibetan was declared the official

---

[12] TCHRD, *Human Rights Update* (August 1999), p. 7.
[13] *A Generation in Peril*, p. 70.
[14] Interview with a freelance reporter for TCHRD in Nepal, November 2005.
[15] *State of Education*, pp. 32, 35; *A Generation in Peril*, pp. 57-59.
[16] *Alternative Report for the Committee on the Rights of the Child*, p.2
[17] *State of Education*, pp. 35, 51.

language of the *TAR*, but it was so only on paper.[18] Chinese is the working language for the government, for the economic life, and for all day-to-day activities.

'Actually the Tibetan language has no value in present-day Tibet. If a letter is mailed with an address written in Tibetan, it wouldn't reach its destination even within Tibet, let alone outside. ... A person who knows only Tibetan will find it difficult even to buy daily necessities. If our language is useless in our own country, where else will it have any use? If the situation remains like this, the Tibetan language will become extinct one day ...'[19]

A pilot project that started in 1989 to experiment with secondary education through the medium of Tibetan for a few schools in different regions was ended in 1996.[20] The Tibetans suffer attacks not only on their language, but also on their religious beliefs. Schools are used as a mechanism for spreading atheism among Tibetans. Indoctrination is very effective on children who, in the process of developing their thoughts and opinions, are easy to manipulate. 'The primary objective of school in Tibet is not to educate the child in its overall development but to indoctrinate the young Tibetan minds with politically correct ideologies.'[21] In 1994 China introduced 'Patriotic education', which involved the daily rising of the Chinese flag in every school and the chanting of the national anthem. It also included study of books and films approved by the authorities. The Party even controls the teaching of history in schools. The history teaching guidelines and textbooks are compiled by committees working under the supervision of the Party.[22]

Ngawang Sangdrol, Human Rights Analyst for *ICT,* asserts:

'Young Tibetans are forced to choose between submitting to the Chinese authorities or retaining their religious, cultural and national identity. Even in their early schooling Tibetan children are ridiculed for their religious beliefs, told that the beliefs of their parents and grandparents are backward. They are told that Tibet has always been a part of China and made to denounce His Holiness the *Dalai Lama* – they are brought up on a lie and anyone who challenges that lie faces abuse, discrimination or worse. Today in Tibet, to wish to protect your language, your culture, your religion is a crime that will either put you in prison or exclude you from an education and a livelihood. This is how a Tibetan child must grow up in Tibet. I am told China ratified the *CRC* in 1992. When a State Party wilfully harms the physical or mental development of a child, it not only degrades the individual child, but also the entire system set up to protect them. I respectfully ask the Committee [of the United Nations on the Rights of the Child] to ensure that China fulfils its legal obligations and puts an end to the

---

[18] TCHRD, *Education in Tibet: A briefing paper for the Special Rapporteur* (May 2003), p. 4.
[19] Words of Khenpo Jigme Phuntsok in his book written in Tibetan, *Thunderous People of the Snowland* (1996), *cited in State of Education*, p. 80.
[20] *State of Education*, p. 50.
[21] Statement of Chen Kuiyuan, former Party Secretary, at the Fifth Regional Meeting on Education in the TAR (26 October 1994), cited in *State of Education*, p. 59.
[22] *State of Education*, p. 52, 58.

use of violence against and indoctrination of children as a tool of political control in Tibet.'[23]

Education in Tibet has never been a priority for the Chinese. In 1976, after the Chinese Revolution, they even shifted financial responsibility for education to the local governments. This affected mostly the poorest regions of Tibet, which were unable to provide elementary education. The Chinese authorities also introduced the so-called 'Hope Project', through which inhabitants were forced to finance the construction, contribute construction materials, and do 'voluntary' labour to build the schools. Since the majority of Tibet's population lives below the poverty line, this system put immense strains on them and deprived them of an education that should be free.

Other reasons for parents to send their children to India are the lack of access to schools due to the great distance between their home and school, sometimes more than an hour by foot, horse or truck, and the lack of quality in education: unqualified teachers do not care whether children learn anything. In rural areas, some schools even lack basic facilities.[24]

'When I lived in Tibet, I used to go to school. The Chinese teachers let us spend all day in the mountains, they didn't teach us anything. They cooked some food for us; it looked like a picnic. Teachers didn't care, even if you didn't attend class. The schools often had no toilets, no water. Doors and windows were broken, so in wintertime it was very cold. Chairs, tables, blackboard were damaged, but nothing was repaired. Chinese have even more facilities, even in the same school they can use computers and Tibetan students cannot.'[25]

'Because of the poor quality, some parents don't want to send their children to school, but then they have to pay high fines, like 5000 *Yuan*. While rich families don't send their own children to school because of the poor level of education, they pay the fees for children of poor families.' '[26]

In 2004, UNICEF Executive Director Ms Carol Bellamy criticized the level of access Tibetan children have to the compulsory 9 years of education,[27] while Ms Katarina Tomasevsky, the UN's Special Rapporteur on Education, called the state of China's education system 'deplorable' for Tibetan people.[28]

---

[23] Testimony of Ms Ngawang Sangdrol, Human Rights Analyst for *ICT*, before the members of the United Nations Committee on the Rights of the Child (UNCRC). Pre-session on China, 6 June 2005.
[24] *State of Education,* p. 26-27, 30.
[25] Interview with a freelance reporter for TCHRD in Nepal, November 2005.
[26] Interview with an Amdo man.
[27] 'UNICEF goes west to help children'. Press statement by Meng Yan. *China Daily,* 3 September 2004.
[28] Commission of Human Rights, 60th Session. The Right to Education. Report submitted by the Special Rapporteur, Katarina Tomasevsky. Addendum: Mission to China. UN Doc E/CN.4/2004/Add.1,Para.36; 21 November 2003.

With Chinese occupation, life in Tibet changed a great deal. Lhasa became a city with bars, cigarettes, prostitution, gambling, and alcohol, and for parents it became more difficult to keep children away from these bad influences.[29]

'In school only Chinese language is taught and bad things, like to take alcohol and cigarettes.'[30]

'Back in Tibet I went to school for four years. I also used to play snooker and flush [a card game], to drink beer, it was a very spoiled life. Now back in India it will be much better. I am going to study really hard.'[31]

'Alcohol and cigarettes are very cheap. In some bars youngsters spend 24 hours drinking with prostitutes and spoiling their life. In Lhasa drugs mainly come from China. Young students bring drugs and guns from Shanghai [China]. They organize parties and then encourage Tibetan youngsters to fight each other. The older ones send the younger ones to steal money and then they buy drugs [heroine] and cigarettes.'[32]

All these reasons force parents to send their children to India, where they have the opportunity to learn classical Tibetan, history, culture and religion.

Occasionally children flee without even informing their parents, because they fear they might oppose the idea.[33]

'I came to the border together with my brother's friend. Nobody knew about my plan, not even my brother.' [34]

---

[29] *A Generation in Peril*, p. 103.
[30] Interview with an Amdo man.
[31] Interview with an 18 year-old boy (see complete interview in chapter 5).
[32] Interview with a freelance reporter for TCHRD in Nepal, November 2005.
[33] *A Generation in Peril*, p. 103.
[34] Interview with a 16 year-old girl (see the complete interview in chapter 5).

CHAPTER 2

HOW MANY CHILDREN FLEE?

'Tous tendaient vers le même but,
un rêve que d'aucuns disaient de fuite,
d'autres de liberté, que certains ne définissaient
même pas et que tous étaient prêts à poursuivre
jusqu'à épuisement de leurs forces,
au péril même de leur vie.'
(Claude B. Levenson, *La Messagère du Tibet*, p. 101)

'All strive for the same goal, a
dream which some call escape, and others
freedom, which some cannot define at all,
and which all are prepared to pursue
to the last of their powers,
even at the risk of their lives.'
(freely translated)

The numbers of refugees over the years have clearly been affected by increased repression in Tibet, increased border control by both Chinese and Nepalese police, and repatriations by the Nepalese. Since the eighties, about 1000 children have arrived in India each year in search of an education. The greatest part of all refugees are children under eighteen.

Immediately after the flight of the *Dalai Lama* in 1959, about 80,000[1] Tibetans followed their spiritual leader into exile. 'They began to pour into the border areas of India, like Assam, Arunchal Pradesh and Sikkim. They were settled by groups of thousands in places like Dharamsala, Dehradun, Karnataka, Orissa and the Darjeeling-Sikkim Himalaya.'[2].

'During the sixties and the seventies however only a small number of refugees arrived in India because till 1979 the border was completely closed, in fact nobody could leave or enter Tibet. Then in 1979 the Chinese policy became more lenient and people could travel to visit their relatives in India or even go into exile. At that time [before 1979] the number of refugees was reduced to only 50 to 100 a year.'[3]

However, due to the first visit of an official delegation of the Tibetan government-in-exile in September 1979, Tibetans learned that in India there were schools under the authority of the *Dalai Lama* where the Tibetan language, culture and history were taught. From that time parents started to send their children to India in massive numbers.[4]

Year after year the number increased: from 100, to 200, to 300. Many Tibetans left their country after the demonstrations organized by the independence movement in Lhasa from September 1987 onwards. To handle the continuing influx of refugees, the United Nations High Commissioner for Refugees (*UNHCR*; see chapter 7) opened an office in Kathmandu in 1991 and started keeping figures.

We had planned to give the monthly numbers of arrived refugees per year in table 1. Although the Chinese might know these precise data, we are, however, reluctant to reveal them. The fact is that during the winter months more refugees take the risk of crossing the Himalayas, since at that time Chinese border patrols are reduced due to the low temperatures (see chapter 4).

[1] Number given by *DIIR of the CTA*. Following the source the number varies between 60,000 and 100,000.

[2] Tanka B. SUBBA, *Flight and Adaptation*, p. 3.

[3] Interview with Mr Lhoudup Dorjee, Director of the Tibetan Refugee Reception Centre in Kathmandu, December 2005.

[4] Sofia STRIL-REVER, *Enfants du Tibet. De cœur à cœur avec Jetsun Pema et sœur Emmanuelle* (Paris, 2000) p. 191.

YEAR	NUMBER
1991	2,046
1992	2,435
1993	3,697
1994	2,542
1995	1,356
1996	2,125
1997	2,236
1998	3,109
1999	2,182
2000	2,319
2001	1,381
2002	1,268
2003	2,257
2004	2,425
2005	3,395
2006	668*

* number on 1 March 2006.

Table 1. Annual number of refugees transiting through Nepal.
Source : Tibet Office Kathmandu.

Over a period of 10 years (1991-2000) the annual figure averaged around 2,300 refugees, with some years showing peaks to more than 3,000 and some troughs.

The number is clearly linked to the political situation of the moment. In the early nineties the situation in Tibet was still very 'explosive': a number of demonstrations took place immediately after the revocation of martial law, and civil disobedience got a footing even in the most remote places. In May and June of 1993 all this agitation peaked in a series of big demonstrations.[5] As the above numbers show, lots of people decided to flee.

Fluctuations in the number of escapees can be explained by changing attitudes on the Chinese and also on the Nepalese side of the border. In 1994 orders were issued by the Chinese government restricting government employees from allowing their children to go to schools in India.[6]

---

[5] On those imprisoned following the 1993 crackdown see Asia Watch, *Detained in China and Tibet. A Directory of Political and Religious Prisoners* (New York, Washington, Los Angeles, London, 1994), pp. 15-17, 33-43.

[6] Tibet Information Network (TIN) News Updates, 3 February 1997, p. 3: '500 children a year seeking education in India'. Unfortunately, due to the closure of TIN in September 2005 their website is now offline.

In 1995 hundreds of Tibetans were repatriated to Tibet from the border with Nepal and even from Kathmandu. The Nepalese government at that time was dominated by the United Marxist League, and the repatriations from Kathmandu appear to have begun shortly after the Nepalese Prime Minister made a visit to Beijing. These repatriations stopped at about the time that a new government led by the Congress Party took over in Nepal.[7]

Despite intensified border security, over the years refugees kept succeeding in getting out of Tibet. In January 2000 the successful flight of the young *Karmapa* Urgyen Trinley, the leader of the Karma-Kagyu school in Buddhism and recognized by the Chinese, was a slap in their face and proved clearly that the so-called religious freedom was an idle word in Tibet.

After his escape the authorities in control of Tibet issued new border regulations, effective from 1 June 2000: Tibetans caught escaping into exile or returning to Tibet from India risked prison sentences of several years.[8]

Moreover, in the fall of 2000 a new checkpoint, a manned border post, was installed on one of the popular escape routes, the Nangpa-la pass, in the Mount Everest region, Solo Khumbu (see chapter 3).[9]

A stricter attitude towards Tibetan refugees was also apparent on the Nepalese side. Nepal was facing a tough period: in June 2001 most of the royal family was murdered by the crown prince, and the Maoist insurgency increased, causing political instability. The last thing Nepal wanted was difficulties with neighbouring China. China is indeed financing a lot of infrastructure, including roads and water supply. In 2001, at least 2,500 Tibetans were arrested on the Tibet/Nepal border according to Xinhua, China's government-run news agency.[10] Of those who did manage to cross into Nepal, several instances were recorded of Nepali police forcefully returning asylum seekers to Tibet, or arresting them for failure to possess travel documents.[11]

Another explanation for the decrease in 2001 was given by the *Central Tibetan Administration (CTA)* in Dharamsala: a lot of refugees did not pass through the *UNHCR* office in Kathmandu during the later months of 2001, but travelled directly to *Bodh Gaya* (north-eastern India) where an important teaching was given in January 2002 by the *Dalai Lama*.[12]

Since 2003, in spite of a heavier Chinese police presence and the deportations from Nepal, the number of refugees has again increased substantially (see table 1).

---

[7] TIN News Updates, 20 December 2000: 'Tibetans sent back across the border as pressure increases in Nepal'.
[8] TIN News Updates, 3 June 2000: 'Tighter regulations, more detentions on Tibet-Nepal border.'
[9] ICT, *Dangerous Crossing: Conditions Impacting the Flight of Tibetan Refugees* (2001), p. 11.
[10] TIN News Updates, 2 January 2002: 'Decline in refugee numbers as China and Nepal tighten security on Tibetan border'. TIN states that this figure could be exaggerated in order to serve Chinese propaganda.
[11] TCHRD Press Release, 7 January 2002, p. 2.
[12] *Dangerous Crossing*, 2001, p. 5.

At the end of 2005 the *TRRC* was, as usual, again crowded during wintertime.

Crowded Reception Centre (TRRC)

An additional reason for this overcrowding was the coming teaching *(Kalachakra)* of the *Dalai Lama* in Amaravati (southern India) in January 2006; thousands of Tibetans left their country to attend this gathering. Not all of them were asylum seekers, many of them returned home after the teaching. At the same time, Nepal's Home Ministry stopped issuing exit permits in November 2005 without any explanation given to the Tibetan authorities. Refugees were stuck at the *TRRC* for several months without proper food or lodging (see chapter 6).

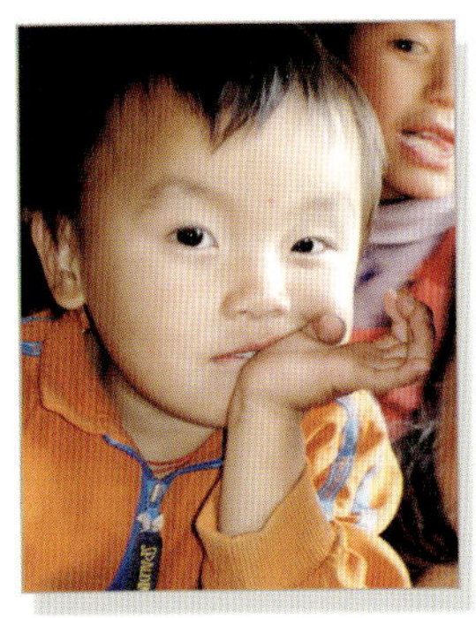

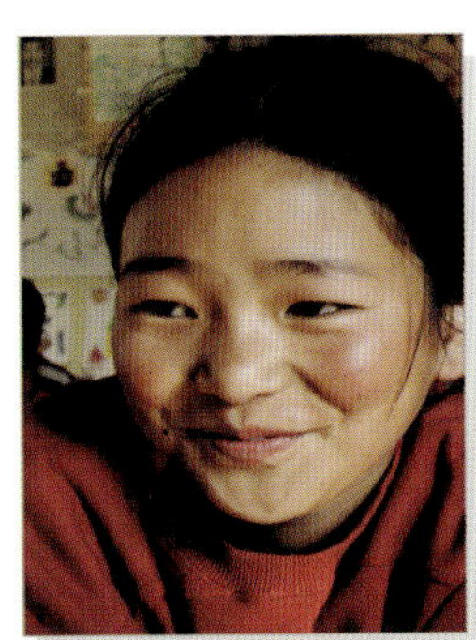

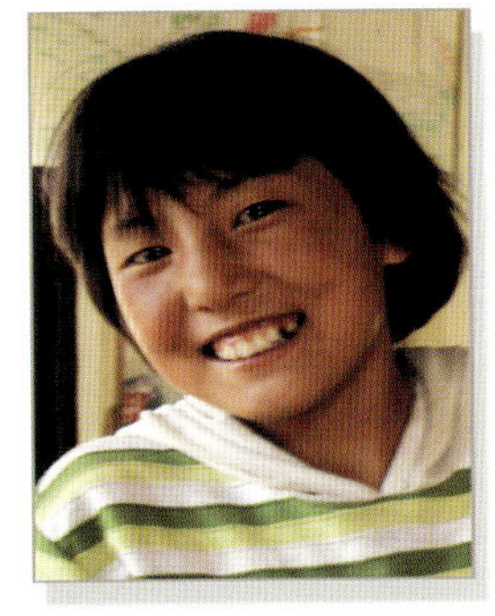
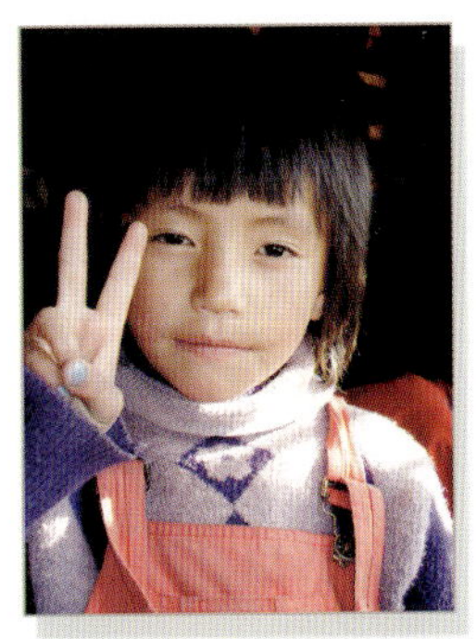
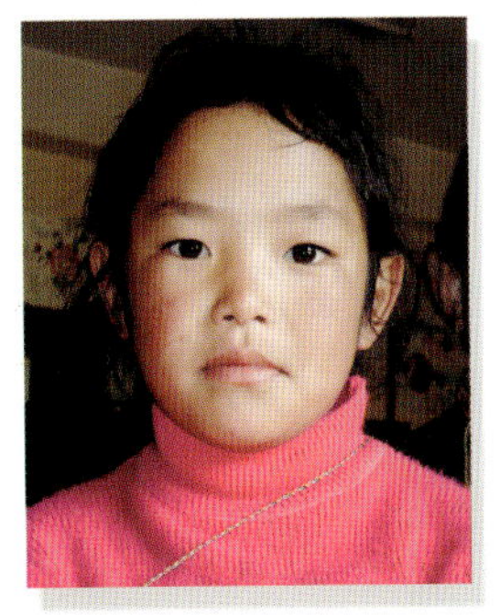
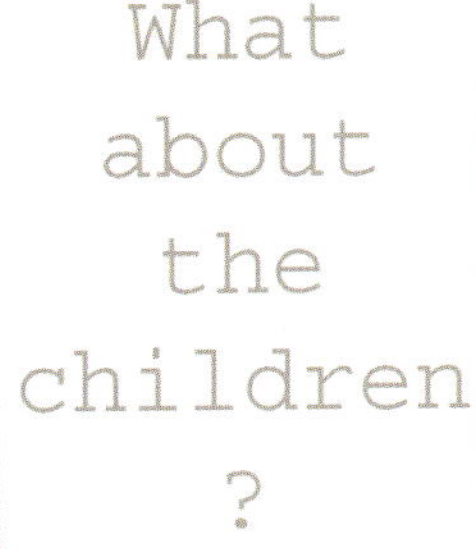
What
about
the
children
?
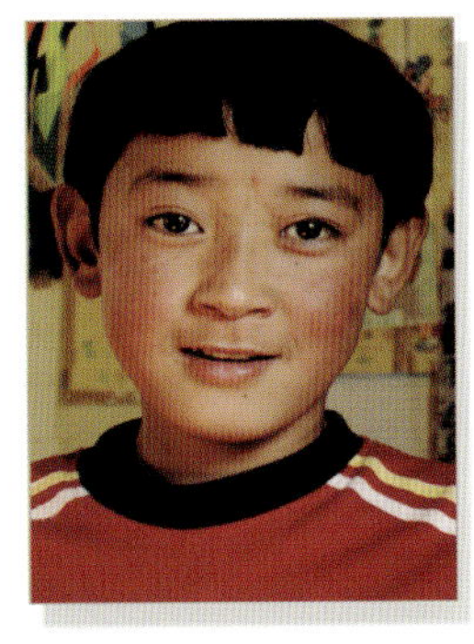

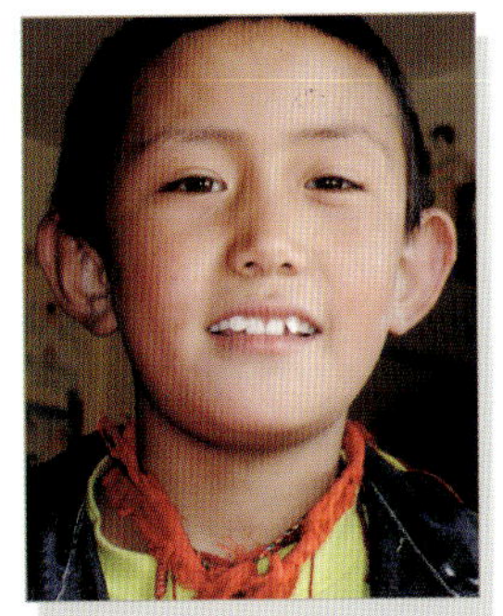
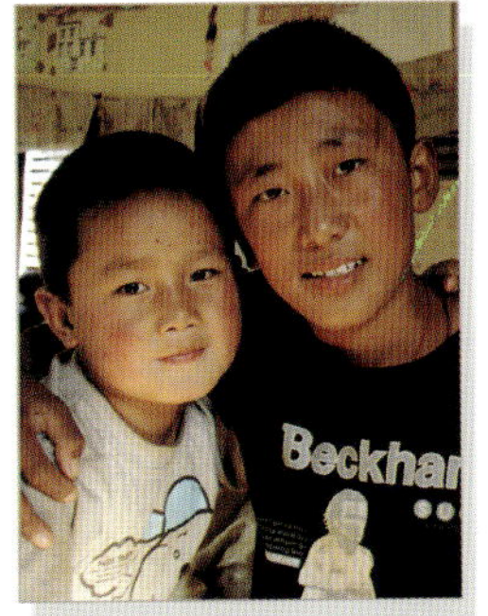

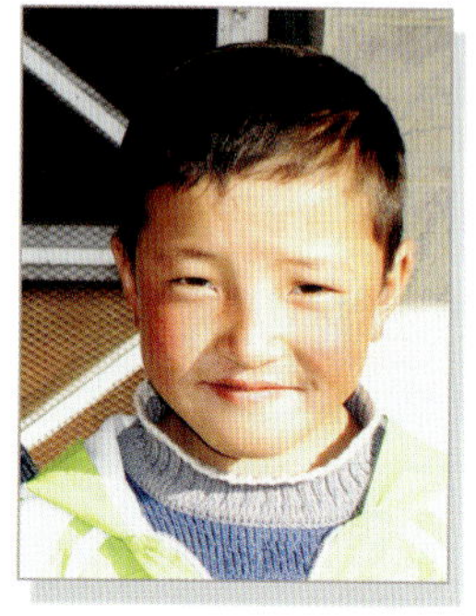

What about the children ?

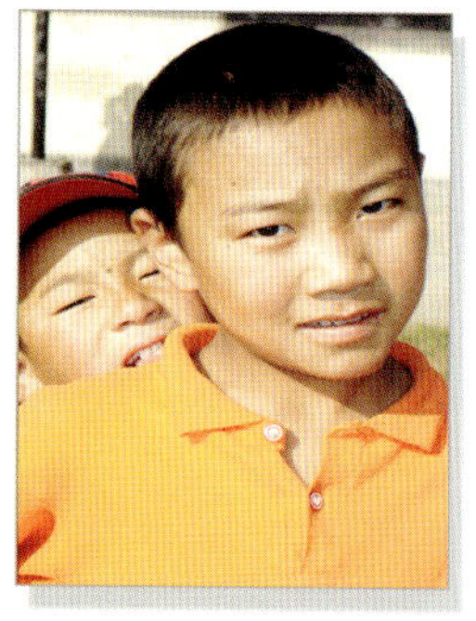

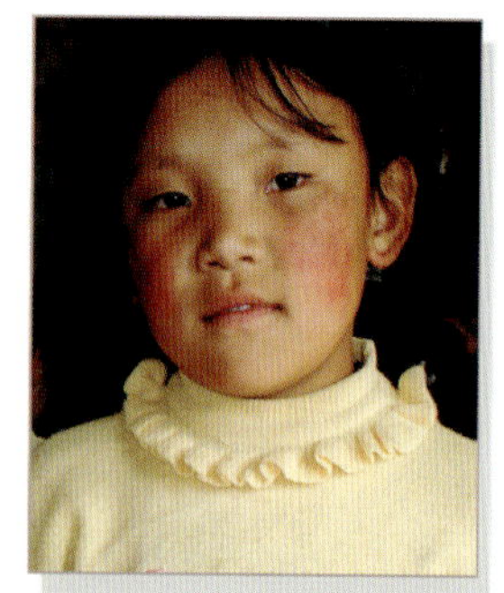

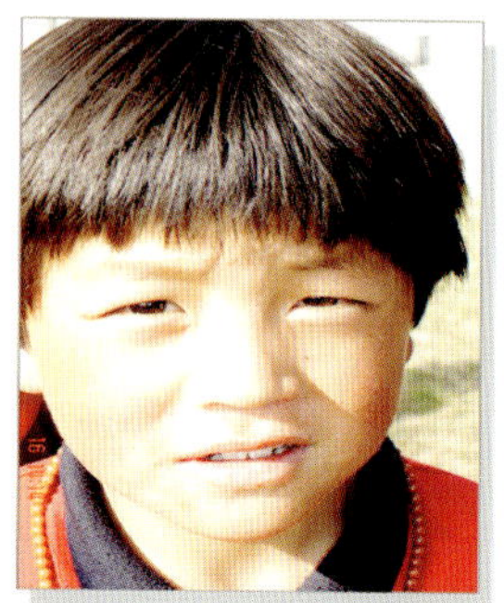

Among the 80,000 Tibetans that followed the *Dalai Lama* into exile in 1959 there were 4,000 children under the age of eight.[13]

In the early eighties, from the moment Tibetans knew there were schools under the authority of His Holiness in India, about 700 children arrived every year. Some of them were babies of only a few months old, most of them however were between five and sixteen years of age.[14]

The share of children under eighteen is on average one-third of the refugees. Many of them have never been to school and most are illiterate.[15]

In fact nobody knows the exact number of those who left Tibet. Hundreds or thousands of children indeed have not succeeded in reaching India: the dead from hunger, cold or exhaustion; those caught by the Chinese or Nepalese police and sent back or put in gaol; and those kept as maids in a Nepalese family once they cross the border (see chapter 4).

Children are the most vulnerable of the refugees and run the greatest risk of dying on their way to freedom. Some of them are even younger than four.

We can only guess how many have lost their lives on the way. Fortunately the statement 'for one that succeeds, two die'[16] seems to be exaggerated.

With a rough average of 700 children arriving in India every year since 1980, nearly 20,000 children may have left their families.

While I was conducting interviews in the *TRRC* in Kathmandu, there were indeed hundreds of children, 80 of them under the age of 13. Many of them attended class to learn the English alphabet, to play, to draw (see chapter 8).

[13] Sofia STRIL-REVER, *Enfants du Tibet*, p. 147.
[14] Sofia STRIL-REVER, *Enfants du Tibet*, p. 191.
[15] *Dangerous Crossing*, 2001, p. 8.
[16] Sofia STRIL-REVER, *Enfants du Tibet*, p. 148.

Classroom in TRRC Kathmandu

List of 62 children attending class in November 2005: [17]

NYIMA YESHI
DOLMA LHAKYI
LHAKPA TSERING
(6 YEARS OLD)
*
TENZIN CHIME
KHANDO TSO
(7 YEARS OLD)
*
NYIMA TSERING
THINLEY CHOEZOM
LOBSANG DEELEN
BHUSANG
RINCHEN TSERING
TENZIN PASANG
DIME WANGMO
DECHEN PALYONG
HARTHO
TSESUNG
THINLEY WANGMO
DECHEN
TSERING CHOTSO
GACHEN DHONDUP
(8 YEARS OLD)
*
BO TSEKA
JAYANG PHUNTSOK
DAWA WOSER
MOTEN LHAMO
PALDEN
LOBSANG DOLMA
NAMGYAL LHAMO
(9 YEARS OLD)
*
SONAM NORBU
TSERING LHAMO
PEMA LHAMO
TENZIN DAWA
YOUGA
PEMA LHAMO
THOGAY NYIMA
(10 YEARS OLD)
*
SONAM WANGMO
DECHEN YATSO
TSERING KYI
(11 YEARS OLD)
*
YESHI DHUNDUP
TASHI TSERING
LOBSANG YESHI
TSERING YANGCHEN
DOLMA
KUNGA DORJEE
TASHI GANTSO
BUCHUNG
LHANTSO
DOLMA
TSERING YANGKYI
GANDEN
(12 YEARS OLD)
*
LOBSANG TSERING
CHOGA PHUNTSOK
LOBSANG TSULTRIM
TENZIN
SONAM WANGMO
KELSANG CHODAK
(13 YEARS OLD)
*
IAYANG DHAKPA
(14 YEARS OLD)
*
TSERING YANTSO
(15 YEARS OLD)
*
TENZIN GUNTSE
TENBA CHOESANG
YESHI
CHOTSO
(17 YEARS OLD)
*
LOBSANG TSEPHU
RINCHEN DHUNDUP
(18 YEARS OLD)

These children come from all different parts of Tibet: Amdo, Chamdo, Kham, Lithang, Lhasa, ... All left their homes in search of education, since most of them had never been to school.

[17] Children are registered the first day they attend class.

CHAPTER 3

ESCAPE ROUTES & CHINESE POLICY

'I avoided following the road,
instead I crossed the mointains and
took shortcuts. It took me 24 days
to reach the border.'
(Anonymous refugee)

To escape from Tibet, Tibetans usually travel by different routes: the one over the Nangpa-la pass is the most common, although more risky since the Chinese installed a manned border post in 2000. An increase in the number of checkpoints, and intensified border control on both sides, have made escape more difficult.

Tibetans who flee their country use different routes depending on the region they come from. In the early seventies Tibetans sometimes fled eastward through Sikkim and Darjeeling (north-eastern India) and thus followed in reverse the routes that the British Colonel Younghusband[1] took during his expedition to Tibet in 1904.[2]

Tibetans escaping from the country often follow the ancient trade routes. Since the eighth century Tibetan and Nepalese traders, nomads, pilgrims and businessmen have crossed the border in both directions. Many of these ancient routes, such as the Nangpa-la, are still used by the Tibetan traders leading their *yak* caravans from Tibet into Nepal. This ancient route connects the town of Tingri to the Nepalese border towns of Namche Bazaar, Lukla and Jiri.[3] In former times Tingri was a crossing of commercial exchanges between Nepali and Tibetans: the Nepali sold their cereals, rice, maize, spices and paper, and purchased wool, salt and animals, such as goats, sheep, horses and *yaks,* from the Tibetans.

Map of Tibet/Nepal border.

'I fled with my mother in 1959. The road we followed was in fact no more than a track on which men used to pass with their *yaks*. The path was covered with snow and we

[1] In 1904 a British expedition invaded and shot its way through to Lhasa to force the rulers of Tibet into formal relations with British India. It came to be known as the Younghusband Mission, after its political officer, the explorer Colonel Francis Younghusband. The attempts of the Tibetans to repel the mission led to their slaughter by the British Indian troops. See Patrick FRENCH, *Younghusband. Last great imperial adventurer* (London, 1994).

[2] Sofia STRIL-REVER, *Enfants du Tibet*, p. 147.

[3] *Dangerous Crossing*, 2004 Update, p. 14.

followed the blood spots of the yaks, whose frozen feet were cracked. Many people fell into crevasses, while others got lost and died.'[4] For me this recollection brought to mind the movie *Himalaya*[5] that tells the story of a family of salt traders. You see images of *yaks* walking on a steep path with a crevasse on one side and the steep mountain on the other. Only one animal passes at a time and still it is very risky.

Even if more details about other routes are known, for the safety of future refugees we will not reveal them here.

One exception can be made for the route across the Nangpa-la pass (5,716 meters above sea level), mentioned earlier and well-known to the Chinese. Here, a manned border post was installed in the autumn of 2000 and the Chinese People's Armed Police (PAP) worked intensively in this area to apprehend Tibetan refugees. According to Xinhua, China's government-run news agency, from February to October 2001 the police tracked and apprehended more than 2,500 people trying to cross the border. This number would presumably include Tibetans returning to Tibet from exile as well as Tibetans detained in border areas without valid documents. The Xinhua report also stated that:

'officers and men of the Tibetan border patrol units had to brave freezing conditions and extreme discomfort in order to carry out their duties of preserving stability in the border regions of the Motherland. As a crossing point, Nangpa-la mountain pass has always been a 'golden route' for people trying to steal across the border. Patrolling the mountain pass is a duty ... that involves a two-hour walk ... they have to wade through waist-deep streams and traverse two mountains that are snow-capped even in summer.'[6]

Nyalam prison near the Tibet/Nepal border.

The PAP is responsible for China's internal security, the protection of state installations, and prisons, and is the primary security presence in the mountain passes. Since 2003 the PAP has tightened border secu-

[4] Information given by Tsering Topgyal (Kathmandu).

[5] *Himalaya*, directed by Eric Valli and produced by Jacques Perrin (1999). In Asia this movie was called *Caravan*.

[6] Xinhua news agency, 16 October 2001, as quoted in TIN News Updates, 2 January 2002: 'Decline in Refugee Numbers as China and Nepal Tighten Security on Tibetan Border'.

rity and access to remote mountain routes. Tibetans caught trying to escape often spend a short time in the Nyalam prison near the border before being sent either to the Snowland New Reception Centre, a prison especially opened for this purpose outside Shigatse in 2003, or to the Nyari prison in Shigatse.[7] To avoid Chinese border guards, refugees often have to make a detour of several days and also travel by night. Crossing the frozen pass then takes another two days.

Even children are sent to prison.

'I was successful in my second attempt to reach the reception centre in Kathmandu. My first attempt was in 2003. I was in a group of 18 people and we were arrested by the Nepalese police who returned us to the Chinese. They sent us to the prison of Shigatse for four months. My brother was with me. Our uncle came and paid 5,000 *Yuan* to release us. The police beat and tortured all the members of our group, except me because I was the youngest.' (Dhundup, now aged 15)[8]

'I saw Chinese border police giving terrible punishment to Tibetans but I was not scared.' (aged 13)

All this happens although the Chinese ratified the CRC, which states that:

'States parties shall take appropriate measures to ensure that a child who is seeking refugee status, receive appropriate protection and human assistance ...' (CRC art. 22) and *'a child shall not be subjected to torture or other cruel, inhuman or degrading treatment or be deprived of his liberty unlawfully or arbitrarily.' (CRC art. 37)*

Violence against refugees became quite common. In August 2005, Chinese border patrol officers opened fire on a group of 51 escapees. The group consisted of monks, nuns and six children. Three of them managed to reach Kathmandu, but the fate of the rest of the group is unknown. It is feared that they might have been arrested. One of the escapees claimed that 30 Chinese border officers, including Tibetan officers, had surrounded them while they were resting. The Tibetan officers threatened to open fire if they attempted to flee. Scared, everybody began to run in different directions. The officers opened fire.[9]

On their way, refugees have to pass a lot of checkpoints, and police control has been intensified on both sides. Once over the border, they still have to pass eight checkpoints on the way to Kathmandu. Some of them arrive there on foot after having walked for three weeks. Others, however, try to reach the nearest village (usually Jiri) and then take the bus to the capital (see chapter 6).[10]

---

[7] *Dangerous Crossing*, 2004 Update, pp. 12-13.

[8] Yangchen's notebook, *TRRC* Kathmandu, 26 September 2005.

[9] TCHRD Human Rights Update, September 2005, p. 1: 'China's border patrol opens fire on a group of fleeing Tibetan refugees'.

[10] Tibet Justice Center (TJC), *Tibet's Stateless Nationals: Tibetan Refugees in Nepal* (Berkeley, Cal., 2002), p. 96.

CHAPTER 4

RISKS

'One girl of 11 years old
carried a younger boy on her back
after he developed severe frostbite
that prevented him from walking;
he eventually died while on her back.'
(*A Generation in Peril,* p. 106)

Escaping across the Himalayas is not without risk: frostbite, hypothermia and physical exhaustion are a few of the physical problems refugee children face. On top of this there is the threat of the Chinese and the Nepalese police who might arrest them, deport them, abuse them ...
Not even the families who send their children are left in peace: they are forced to get their children back from India by threats that they risk losing their job, or their house.

Let us try to imagine what it means for a small child, sometimes under the age of four, to undertake a trip from Tibet, the world's largest and highest plateau (over 3,000 metres above sea level), across the Himalayas, the world's highest mountain range.

High altitude means very low temperatures, thin air and sharp wind. The refugees seldom wear appropriate clothes or shoes, let alone sunglasses to avoid snow blindness. They carry almost no luggage, no spare clothes or shoes, not even dried yak dung to light a fire, afraid of attracting the attention of the Chinese police in towns on their way.

Two-thirds flee during the winter season, since due to the icy temperatures they have the great advantage of less control by the Chinese. Most of the time they travel by night to avoid being seen. They have no alternative to travelling in winter since in springtime the differences between day and night temperatures are big and in summer there is the monsoon. In spring the snow melts due to the mild temperatures, but at night temperatures go down and wet shoes and clothes freeze to their small bodies. In summer during the monsoon there is heavy rainfall which reduces visibility and makes the rivers swollen and unfordable.[1]

Possible risks at high altitude.

1. Hypothermia is defined as a reduction in the core temperature of the body to below 35°C. Acute hypothermia follows a sudden drop in body temperature over minutes or hours, as occurs with immersion in cold water or a sudden climatic change. Sub acute or chronic hypothermia results from a gradual drop in core temperature over hours to days. In a mountain environment this typically occurs in the setting of inadequate clothing or shelter between 32 and 35°C, while a core temperature less than 32°C represents severe hypothermia. Children and lean young men are at particular risk. (...) Cold exposure is a particular risk for children on mountains. There is an increased risk for the exhausted child who is carried by an adult and who fails to wear adequate clothing. A child who is being carried is indeed not generating heat and at low ambient temperatures will need extra layers of clothing even when the adult who is carrying him is comfortably warm.

[1] *Dangerous Crossing*, 2001, p. 11.

2. Snow blindness. In snowscapes reflected sun can be very intense. This can result in snow blindness up to 4 hours after exposure if appropriate sunglasses with UV filter are not worn. It results in a gritty, painful eye with an oedematous eye-lid and cornea together with conjunctival oedema and hyperaemia. The pain is intense.

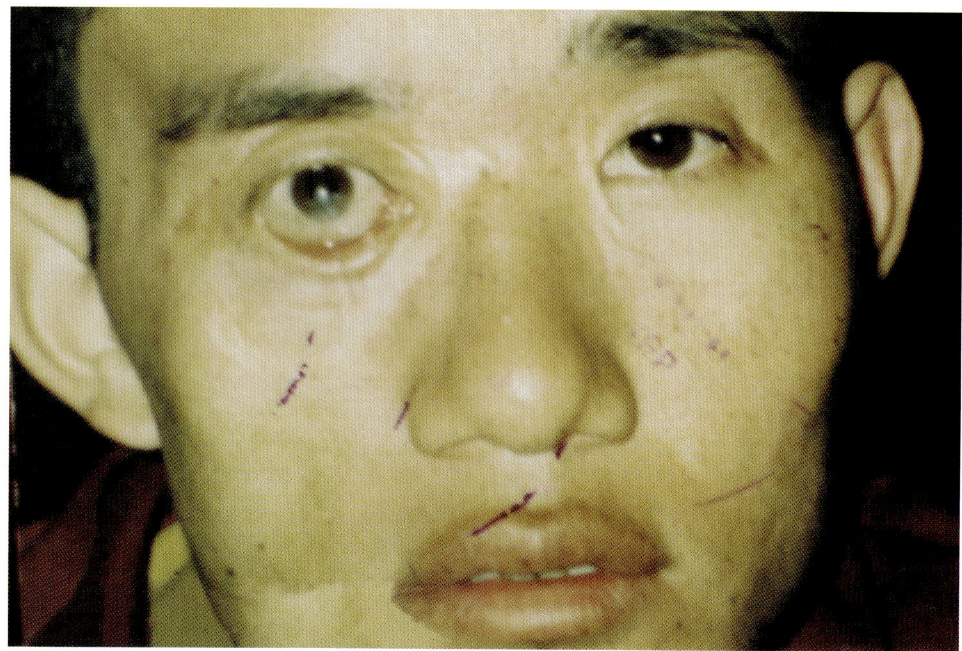

Snow blindness - Picture on the wall of the TRRC clinic

3. Frostbite occurs at temperatures below zero and is due to freezing with consequent death of tissues. The risk of frostbite depends both on the environmental temperature, the wind chill factor and the length of exposure. It can affect any area, but is especially common in the hands and feet. It may also affect the face (nose, chin, earlobes, cheeks, lips).There are three stages: frost-nip when the skin becomes white and loses sensation, but remains viable. Complete return of sensation may take weeks.

Superficial frostbite when both skin and subcutaneous tissues are involved. The skin is initially pale and cold, but the underlying deep tissues remain undamaged. Blisters usually develop within one or two days and resolve to form a black carapace. The carapace is denervated and painless and separates from viable tissue along a sharp line of demarcation after several weeks.

Deep frostbite, the deeper structures are affected, including muscle, tendons and occasionally bone. The affected part is insensitive and hard. Blisters develop and eventually gangrene with inevitable tissue loss.'[2]

[2] Quoted in extenso from Andrew J. POLLARD & David R. MURDOCK, *The High Altitude Medicine Handbook* (Micro Edition, India, 1997), pp. 40, 45-46, 48-49, 54.

'The road was blocked by thick snow, so we had to wait for one day in the mountains. Some people of my group had frostbite on their feet; I only had a minor wound.' (aged 9)

The previous 'medical' explanation of frostbite remains quite theoretical and difficult to imagine if you have never seen it in reality. Until recently I had only read stories about frost-bitten refugees and seen pictures of their feet, but in the TRRC hospital I sat next to a girl with two heavily mutilated feet. Seeing her painful face while she was carefully taking off the bandages that were sticking to the open wounds, it suddenly became cruelly real.

'I was in a bigger group, but then we had to walk through the snow. The snow was reaching to hip height, so our guide advised us to go back. Everybody returned except five of us, we did not want to go back. For four days we walked in the snow, and then it took us 11 more days to reach here. I was lucky because I only have minor frostbite. I need to take antibiotics and they clean the wounds every day. One lady is now in the hospital, she was in a bad condition, and they have to amputate both her feet.'[3]

'Every day we soak their feet in warm water with betadine, an antiseptic for the disinfection of the tissues. After two or three days of treatment, a demarcation line between the dead part and the good part appears. Then we know where they have to amputate the feet. The worst case is already admitted to

Little girl bathing her frostbitten feet

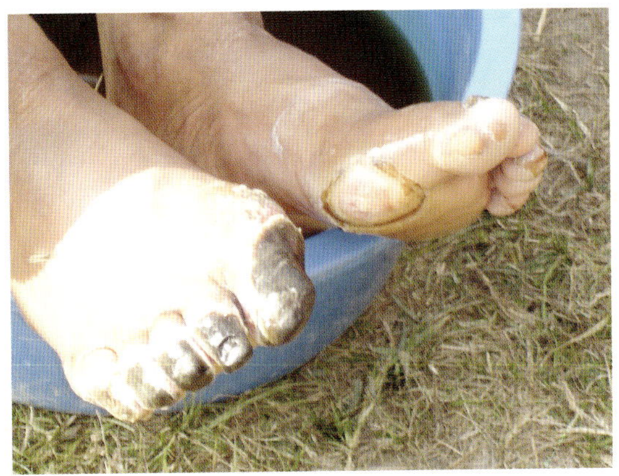

A boy's feet

[3] See complete interview in chapter 5.

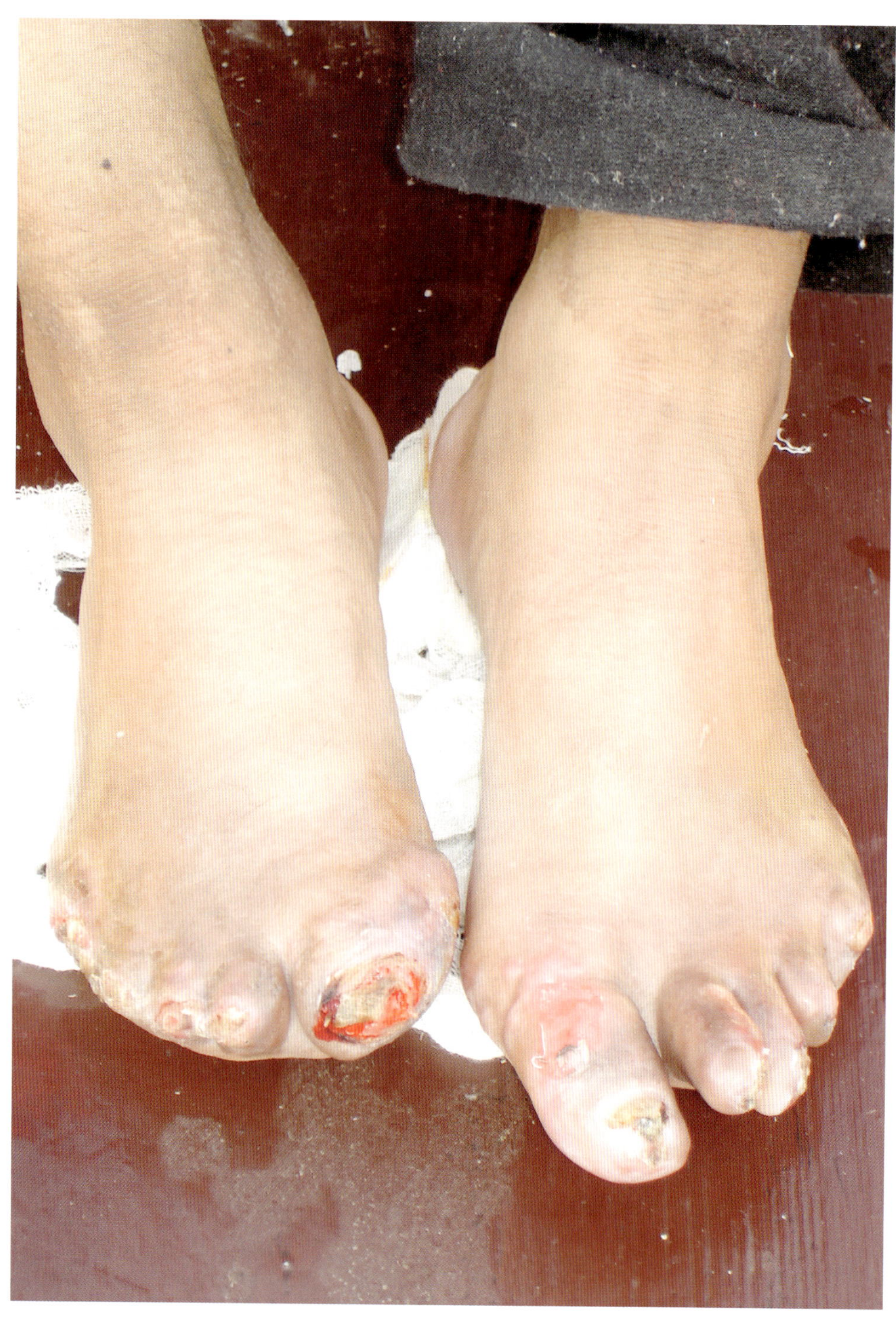

Feet after amputation
TRRC Kathmandu, 1 February 2006

the hospital: her two feet needed amputation. The less severe cases need treatment with warm water and betadine for several months, they slowly recover.'[4]

'For two or three days we had to walk in the snow, sometimes the snow reached to our knees, sometimes to our armpits. Luckily we had warm clothes and we wore plastic bags over our trousers to protect our legs, so none of us had frostbite. We heard stories of other Tibetans who on their way faced big difficulties, like frostbite of toes and fingers. One girl from Amdo she died, she was frozen to death.'[5]

One of the refugees of this group took the two following pictures.

A group of refugees on their way to freedom.

'The snow reached sometimes to our knees.'

Examples of physical injuries due to the harsh climate are legion. Some children die of cold, exhaustion, hypothermia or illness.

'A 13 year old girl died while trying to escape from Tibet, it was her third attempt to flee to India. Her first attempt had failed early last year when she was arrested by the police at Shigatse, 220 km from Lhasa. On her second attempt she had been arrested at Sakya, 80 km further from Shigatse but still 120 km north of the border. The girl, whose name was Deyang or "melodious happiness", was travelling with a group

[4] Interview with Tenzin Yangkyi, health-worker in TRRC Kathmandu, November 2005.
[5] See complete interview in appendix 2.

of 14 other refugees. By the time the escapees reached the Nangpa-la the girl was suffering from the cold and had developed a lung infection. "She was coughing and could not walk, so all the people in the group took turns carrying her, wrapped in a blanket," added a farmer who was with the escape group. 48 hours after they crossed the border into Nepal, Deyang died. Her body was buried by the other members of the group and prayers were recited by the monks.

A boy of the same age died in Kathmandu as a result of injuries received during the flight across the mountains. Tsering Phuntsog had been part of a large group of 111 escapees which was caught in a storm on the Larkya Pass, 55 km north-east of Annapurna (a range of 8000m peaks). The escapees had to walk through waist-deep snow before they reached Nepali villages where local police helped them to safety and then escorted them to Kathmandu. At least 43 of the group had to be treated there for frostbite, and three boys were the most serious cases and had to have their toes or feet amputated. Tsering Phuntsog died shortly after a minor operation carried out at a public hospital in Kathmandu nearly a month after the amputation. The child appears to have been severely traumatized by the experience in the mountains, even before the amputation. "He was still shivering from the cold and looked very ill," said a Westerner who saw Tsering Phuntsog the day after he was brought to Kathmandu. "He didn't want to speak to anyone, and he looked extremely disturbed and scared," she recalled.'[6]

Sometimes injuries from slipping and falling, or illness, can lead to being abandoned by a guide who does not want to put at risk the whole group for one child. Also pregnant women are often abandoned, because they are not able to follow the pace of the group.

'I came with a group of 27 people. One family of 3 persons had to stay behind because their daughter fell ill.' (aged 7)

'On the trip I was sick and I cried a lot. I missed my mother a lot.' (aged 9)

'I was in a group of 108 people, one man got sick. Blood was coming from his mouth and he had frostbite on both his feet. We waited for 2 days but then the guide decided to leave him behind.'[7]

In 2003 a 17 year-old girl fell into a crevasse on the Nangpa-la pass. Her companions tried to rescue her by means of a rope made from their clothes. In spite of their efforts the rope broke...[8]

On the way food is rarely available, so refugees are even forced to eat grass or snow!

[6] TIN News Updates, 3 February 1997: 'Two children die in Mountain Escape Bid'. See also TIN News Updates, 15 February 1997: 'Three more die in escape attempt'. TCHRD Human Rights Update, February 1998: 'Five children die in fleeing Tibet'. TCHRD Human Rights Update, December 2001: 'Death of a baby during treacherous winter crossing'.
[7] See complete interview in chapter 5.
[8] *Dangerous Crossing*, 2003 Update, p. 15.

Many of them suffer from stomach problems and eating snow can cause ulcers.[9] Some of the refugees told me that they walked for days without having any food. Others are able to buy *tsampa* (roasted barley flour) from Tibetans on the way.

'It took me 6 days to cross the mountains. I had no food for 3 days.' (aged 15)

Apart from these hazards, the biggest risk is apprehension by the Chinese police. In the previous chapter we already mentioned the increased security and control measures. Crossing the border without a visa is a violation of article 322 of China's Criminal Law (1997) that states:

Whoever violates the laws and regulations controlling secret crossing of the national boundary (border), and when the circumstances are serious, shall be sentenced to not more than one year of fixed-term imprisonment and criminal detention or control.

Refugees who ended up in a Chinese prison report that most individuals caught at the border receive a sentence of three to five months, during which beatings and torture with an electric baton are common. They are also made to perform hard labour.

Although they travel during the night to reduce the risk, many are caught by the police. Even pregnant women are not safe. A pregnant woman who had been imprisoned gave birth while she was in detention. In 2003 I met her son in the nursery of *TCV* Dharamsala. He looked very sad and was sitting silently in the corner of the room, while the other children were playing.

Little boy born in prison. TCV Dharamsala.

[9] Interview with Tenzin Yangkyi, health-worker at *TRRC* Kathmandu, November 2005.

Maltreatment and interrogation are routine procedures for refugees who get caught.

'We were beaten with electric batons and we were sent back to Lhasa and imprisoned for several months.'[10] Even children are detained and tortured.

Gyaltsen Pelsang, a 13 year-old who escaped into exile and arrived in India on 18 December 1996, walks with a prominent limp. She is the living proof of Chinese atrocities against juvenile prisoners. While in detention, she was made to stand for hours on a cold floor. This, in combination with the beatings she endured during her interrogation, has permanently damaged her right leg.[11]

Chinese officials also gave bounties to local people who provided information on Tibetans suspected of planning to escape across the Nangpa-la.[12]

'The Chinese in the border area, they give money to the nomads, Tibetan as well as Nepalese who are living there. They have to watch around and when they catch a child, they get a certain amount of money. They report it to Chinese officer, then the police they catch the child and bring it back.'[13]

Nepalese border guards started having friendly relations with their counterparts on the other side of the border. For handing back Tibetan refugees they can earn commission.[14] On 31 May 2003 a group of 18 Tibetans was sent back by force from Kathmandu. This repatriation attracted the international attention of Amnesty International, the European Union, and several *NGOs*, and was widely covered by the press.[15] Eyewitnesses described the refugees as being carried crying and screaming into vehicles before being driven in the direction of the border. The three smallest children, two girls aged nine and six, and a six year-old boy, had been released into the custody of *UNHCR* and were not deported. It was the first time refugees were deported from Kathmandu (see also chapter 6).

Several cases of rape have also been reported. While there are few reports of rapes by police in Tibet, Nepalese police in border areas seem to be more often involved in the sexual assault of Tibetan women.

---

[10] TIN News Updates, 20 December 2000, p. 3: 'Tibetans sent back across the border as pressure increases on Nepal'.

[11] *Alternative Report for the Committee on the Rights of the Child*, p. 25.

[12] TIN News Updates, 2 January 2002, p. 1: 'Decline in refugee numbers as China and Nepal tighten security on Tibetan border'.

[13] Interview with freelance reporter TCHRD in Nepal, November 2005.

[14] TIN News Updates, 20 December 2000, p. 3: 'Tibetans sent back across the border as pressure increases on Nepal'.

[15] Amnesty International Press Release, 2 June 2003: 'Nepal: Forcible return of Tibetans to China unacceptable'; Kate Saunders, 'Update on Tibetan deportees: Nepal, China issue statements' (7 June 2003) <http://www.freetibet.org/press/specialreport070603.html>; 'Nepalese Government Bows to Chinese Pressure: Tibetan Refugees in Nepal Face Imminent Deportation to Tibet' (Tibet Justice Center Release, 29 June 2003), <http://www.tibetjustice.org>; 'Déclaration de la présidence au nom de l'Union Européenne sur l'expulsion de 18 demandeurs d'asile du Népal vers la Chine' (Comité de Soutien au Peuple Tibétain – France, Tibet Info du 25 Juin 2003), <http://www.tibet-info.net>.

'We were five men and two girls, one aged 13 and the other 16. After crossing the border we reached the woods of the Tatopani area (near the Nepalese border). A group of eight men dressed in Nepali police uniform, armed with knives, suddenly attacked us. The girls were stripped naked in front of us and the men raped both of them in turn. Some of the men raped the girls repeatedly.' [16]

The Nepalese police often ask the children for bribes, steal their few belongings, beat them or abuse them physically before allowing them to go.[17] *TIN* even reports an incident where two children were shot, wounded, and robbed of their possessions.[18]

In the stories I have read and heard in the *TRRC* (see chapter 5) a lot of refugees face the same problems with the Maoists or with the Nepalese army. Moreover, often they wear civilian clothes, so it is difficult for the escapees to recognize their aggressors.

'When we arrived at Lukla, we met some people; they took our money and our clothes. Some of us were beaten. Two of them held me down on the ground and sexually harassed me by touching my upper body. I have been crying a lot. It also happened to three other girls. It took place where nobody could see us, behind the trees.' (aged 12)

'At the border we were stopped by the Nepali police. We were beaten and they told us to go back to Tibet. They threatened us with their guns and they beat the elder people. They finally took our money and our clothes.' (aged 13)

'The Nepalese army men told us to go back. Then they arrested us. They checked our bags while pointing a gun at our head. I cried a lot because I was very afraid. (aged 10)

'Our group was arrested by five Maoists who took us to a Maoist camp. There were a lot of them, they checked through our luggage and took a man's watch and 8,000 *Yuan*. Then they asked for 80,000 *Rupees*. I had 20 *Yuan* in my pocket but they didn't find it. Finally after having paid 2,000 *Yuan* we were released. Then the Nepali police caught us and kept us for one night. We had to pay 40 *Rupees* each for food and accommodation.' (aged 11)

'Sometimes there is misunderstanding between the Nepalese police and Tibetans and they start fighting. We don't know exactly what happened, but the police started shooting and this man [she points to a picture] died on the spot, they shot him in his head. Another man was shot in his right side and it came out in the middle of his back, luckily it did not hit his lungs. But it took him one year to recover. One girl was also wounded and had all the bones in her leg damaged; she needed two years to recover.'[19]

---

16 TCHRD Human Rights Update, November 2004: 'Minors raped enroute to exile'. Other reports: TIN News Updates, 16 February 1999, 'Tibetan girls raped by Chinese police'. TIN News Updates, 26 February 1997, 'Tibetan refugee raped 12 times by Nepalese police'.

17 *A Generation in Peril*, p. 107.

18 TIN News Updates, June 1993.

19 Interview with Tenzin Yangkyi, health-worker at *TRRC* Kathmandu, November 2005.

Even on the way from the border to Kathmandu refugees risk being caught by the police. Since the Maoist insurgency eight police checkpoints have been established on the road to the capital. Newly arrived Tibetans who do not speak a word of Nepali are easy prey. Some youngsters were caught by the police only a few minutes away from the *TRRC* and taken to prison. Penalties can be high. If the refugee is not able to pay the fine, he has to stay in prison for several months (see one of the interviews in chapter 5).

As if all this is not enough, even the families who have sent their children to India face problems. Parents are threatened with monetary fines, sometimes up to 6,000 *Yuan*,[20] freeze in promotion and salary increase, and forfeiting the residential permits of their children. This is an intensification of the mid-1994 ban when government employees were instructed to bring their children back from Tibetan schools in India within 3 months. It started as a general instruction but was later imposed as a regulation resulting in 37 children returning to Tibet.[21]

Even people working in the tourist sector and having contact with foreigners,[22] and later anyone whose children were studying in India, could lose their job, their house and even get arrested if they did not get their children back. In spite of these threats, parents continue to send their children to India. Only 75 parents came to India to fetch their children.[23]

---

[20] A mother from the region of Shigatse was fined 6,000 *Yuan* for taking her 3 children to school in India. See TCHRD Human Rights Update, May 2004: 'Poor education and discriminatory practices in Tibet make children go into exile. Monetary fines for sending children to Tibetan schools in India.'

[21] TCHRD Press Release, 14 August 2000.

[22] Claude B. LEVENSON, *La Messagère du Tibet. Le Retour du panchen-lama* (Arles, 1997), pp. 68-69.

[23] Sofia STRIL-REVER, *Enfants du Tibet,* p. 190.

CHAPTER 5

INTERVIEWS

To the ones that did not survive
their flight to freedom.

Depending on the point of departure in Tibet, the journey can take some weeks or even more than a month. Mostly people gather in Lhasa and continue from there as a group, relying on a guide. When a group is caught, the longest sentence is reserved for him. Most of the guides are trustworthy persons, but sometimes they turn their group over to the Chinese, abandon individuals, or disappear when the group meets the police.

Escaping from Tibet can take a few weeks or sometimes more than a month, it depends on the place where the would-be refugee sets off from, and on whether he takes a bus or a truck or does it all by foot.

'From my county to Lhasa we walked for 15 days, then from Lhasa to Kathmandu it took us one month and 10 days by foot.'[1]

'It took me four months to get here, but I was not afraid.' (aged 11)

Generally people gather in Lhasa where some of them try to earn money for the journey. Then they search for a group to join and look for a guide. Actually, the success of the escape into exile largely depends on the presence of an experienced guide. Since he regularly brings refugees across the border, he is best placed to help avoid Chinese border security, to cross the difficulties of the mountainous terrain and to find the right way.

His first job consists in recruiting candidate refugees. In recent years guides went to eastern Tibet, especially areas in Gansu and Sichuan, searching for groups of individuals who wish to flee.[2]

'I stayed three months in Kyirong since the guide went out to look for more people. Most of the day I stayed in the room, because I was so scared.' (aged 13)

Refugee groups range in size from only a few to twenty or more. Last November a group of 108 people escorted by two guides arrived successfully in Kathmandu. The larger the group, however, the greater the danger of being apprehended on the way by border security.

The guide has to be paid in full in advance. The price can vary, as can be read in the following interviews, but for a lot of refugees this amount represents a year's salary or all their savings. Most refugees hire guides to accompany them to the border or a short distance into Nepal. The Chinese call them 'people smugglers' and have imposed stiff prison sentences on them.[3] When a group is caught by the police the longest sentences are indeed reserved for the guides or the organizers of the group. Some guides stopped their 'activities' because they became too frightened of the increased control after the forced repatriation of May 2003.

---

[1] See complete interview further in this chapter.
[2] *Dangerous Crossing*, 2001, p. 13.
[3] *Dangerous Crossing*, 2001, pp. 12-13.

Most of the guides are trustworthy individuals who really take care of their group.

'I came with two other children and one nun. It was very cold and I felt very tired and scared. My two friends were smaller than me and the guide carried them over the mountains.' (aged 8)

'On the way I saw a lot of soldiers and I was so scared. We ran away from them and the guide was holding my hand.' (aged 12)

However, guides are sometimes forced to abandon members of the group who are ill or wounded, in order not to put the whole group at risk (see interview further in this chapter).

A particularly poignant story is that of Dorje Tseten, aged 5, whose grandmother paid a fortune to two guides but who was abandoned by them while asleep. Nearly frozen to death, he was luckily rescued by a helicopter of two American tourists. He survived, but his ten toes had to be amputated.[4]

Refugees complain that guides often leave them behind when they meet the Nepalese police. There have also been reports of guides cheating them by turning them over to the Public Security Bureau (i.e. the Chinese authorities) in Lhasa or Shigatse.[5]

'I came with my younger brother, two other children and two adults. Our guide cheated us, took our money and ran away. It took us almost one month to walk through the mountains. It was very cold. We did not get food for five days.' (aged 13)

Across the border, refugees often get local Nepalese to escort them. Ascertaining the number of Nepalese who work as guides only on the Nepal side of the border is difficult, but the number is likely not to exceed fifty. The cost for a Nepalese guide is between $80 and $350.[6]

On their way refugees also meet Nepalese who propose their help in exchange for money. Not all of these individuals are well-intentioned, as is apparent from some of the stories that follow.

It is thought that refugees with a guide have more chance of arriving safely than those without a guide. However, Manuel Bauer, a Swiss photographer and close friend of the *Dalai Lama*, made a journey with a father and his six year-old daughter from Lhasa to Dharamsala. They managed it without a guide and in only twenty-one days.[7] A few children I have met also succeeded in escaping on their own.

---

[4] Sofia STRIL-REVER, *Enfants du Tibet*, pp. 68-69.
[5] *Dangerous Crossing*, 2001, p. 14.
[6] *Dangerous Crossing*, 2001, p. 13.
[7] Manuel BAUER, 'Du Tibet à Dharamsala', *GEO magazine* (November 1995), pp. 123-134.

While interviewing these children, I encountered several problems. First of all there was the language barrier. I do not speak Tibetan and newly arrived refugees from Tibet mostly do not speak any English at all. This problem was resolved by a few of my Tibetan friends who helped me with the translation. However, they too did not understand some dialects. Then one person translated the Amdo into the Tibetan of Lhasa, the so-called classical Tibetan, and then this was translated to me. One girl I was not able to interview because I could not find anybody who understood her dialect.

Another problem is that most of them had never travelled before. Sometimes they could simply not tell the name of the places they had passed because they had never been there before. It was sometimes very difficult to obtain clear details, because they have never been to school and are illiterate.

'I never went to school, but I worked with my father in the fields. We had *yaks* and sheep. I cannot say if I took the bus in Lhasa, since I don't know the names of the cities I have passed. All I know is that from my home it took me three days by truck, then two more days in a pick-up and 15 days of walking.'[8]

When the Nepalese police asked one girl if she was from Tibet, she answered 'No, I am from Amdo.' She did not even know it was a part of Tibet. Some of the children were also afraid and did not want me to take their picture. They were confused because they did not know who they could trust. I was told that there were indeed spies in the reception centre. And like most of the Tibetan youngsters some of them were very shy. It was only after spending a lot of time with them that they started talking.

Since we publish their picture, we have deliberately omitted the names and the place of residence of each interviewed child to protect them and their family members still in Tibet.

My first interview took place in Dharamsala in 2003. The story pushed me to write this book.

'We were nomads and we were living in a small town in Kham. In April 2002, me, my husband and our five year-old fled with a group of 28 persons from different regions. For 350 *Yuan* per person a truck brought us to Lhasa in eighty-four hours. We lived for one month with our relatives, waiting for the OK of the 'agency' to leave. After having paid 800 *Yuan* to the guide, a truck brought us to Shigatse during the night. From there we had to walk for two hours to reach Lhatse. We had to cross the bridge, while there was a jeep waiting for us at the other side. When 20 minutes later we got out of the overloaded jeep, it was found that two boys of nine and ten years old had been crushed to death. We had to move on. Most of the time we travelled by night and rested during the day to avoid Chinese controls. We ate *tsampa* with butter and drank tea made from tea leaves, butter, and salt. The next night we had to cross a mountain one by one since there was a Chinese camp in the neighbourhood. 20 persons succeeded, but unfortunately my husband and my son were captured together with some others. I had no choice; I could not go back because this meant betraying

[8] Interview with a 17 year-old boy, November 2005.

the whole group. So we continued to walk all night. Arriving at the Nepalese border in the region of Solu Khumbu, I had only little money left to buy some food. In Jiri we were taken to the police prison for three days and after that we walked for two weeks to Kathmandu. In total we walked for two months. In the *TRRC* we stayed for 21 days to recover. I didn't suffer from frostbite but I had lost a lot of weight. When later on I arrived in Dharamsala, I realized I was pregnant, so I couldn't go to the Transit School were other young Tibetan refugees are admitted [see chapter 9]. Luckily I got some financial help from a few monks and a young man.'[9]

Touched by this story, I asked Amnesty International if they could do something to help find the missing husband and son, but my request failed. 'I am afraid I have no further news to report to you so far. A major problem for us is that it is very difficult to contact people directly in Tibet/China as that can put them at further risk. This makes it very difficult to obtain accurate information'.[10]

The *Convention on the Rights of the Child* seems to be non-existent...

For some children the crossing went smoothly, they encountered no major problems on the road, met no police or Maoists, did not fall ill or suffer frostbite. When I asked them about their journey, it was as though they were telling me about an ordinary trip. The smallest of them indeed have no idea to what extent their life will change.

A 7 year-old boy from Lhasa (left) went to school for one year in Tibet. He came to the border by jeep, together with his brother, uncle and aunt. From there they walked by foot for one night and one day. They faced no problems. He only had to cross a river while somebody else held a rope across the river.

[9] Interview with a 25 year-old woman.

[10] Email from Mr Mark Alison of the East Asia Team of Amnesty International (London), 25 February 2004.

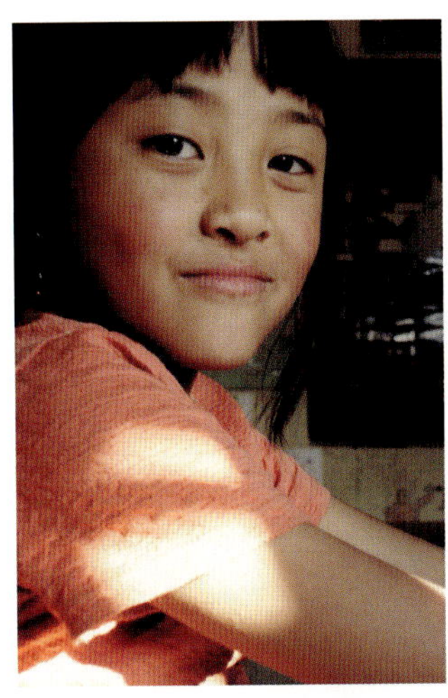

A 10 year-old girl from Amdo had never been to school in Tibet. She travelled with a Nepalese guide, who is married to an Amdo girl. She arrived in Lhasa and from there they took a bus for four days. Then they had to walk for one night. She didn't meet other people nor have any problem on her trip; her guide didn't even ask her for money.

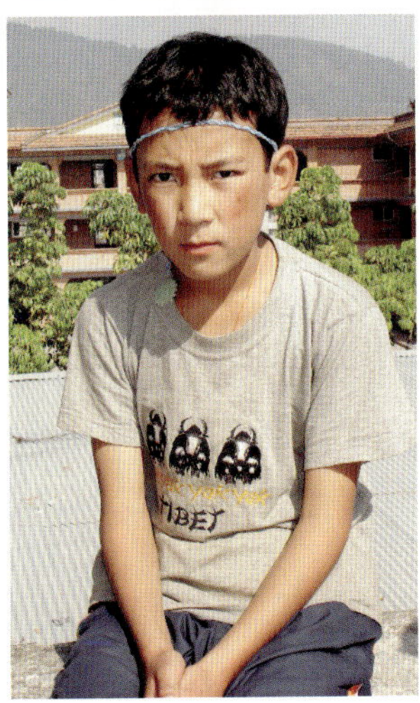

An 11 year-old boy from Kham never went to school in Tibet. He came with his brother and they travelled together with a guide. From Lhasa to Dram they took a bus, they had no problem reaching the border. Then they had to walk for one week. He thinks that only at the border was it a bit dangerous...

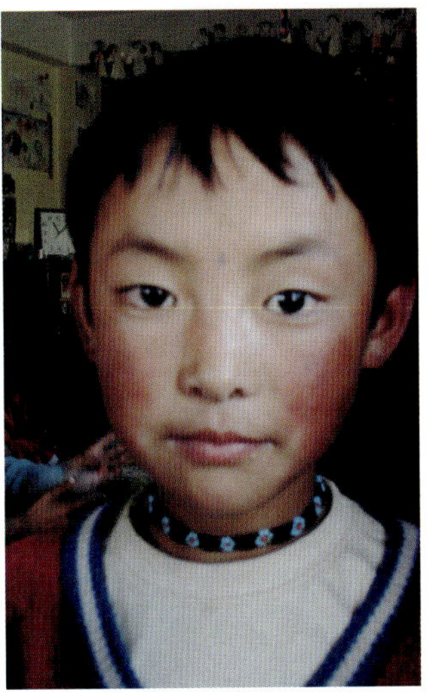

An 8 year-old girl from Kham never went to school in Tibet. She came in a small group of four children: one girl smaller than her, one taller and one boy. They took a bus to Lhasa and from there another bus to Dram. Then they walked for three days, day and night, through the forest with a Nepalese guide.

As has been said before, some children manage to escape all by themselves, without a guide.

Two boys, 13 and 15, from the region of Mount Kailash.

'We came only the two of us without guide. From our city to the Nepalese border we came by walking. Then from the border we took a bus. In total it took us three months to reach here.
[And what about your feet?]
Now they are fine, but we had some problems because of too much walking and we had also some injuries from the shoes.
[Frostbite?]
Luckily no frostbite.
[How did you manage since you had no guide to tell you the way?]
Someone from Lhasa had written the name of some places on a paper and we just followed this map.
[Did you also walk during the night-time?]
Some nights we walked, but most of the time we walked during daytime.
[And what about the food?]

We brought *tsampa*. On the way we met some Tibetans and we asked them for some food and from them we also received *tsampa*.
[Did you meet other groups on the way?]
Yes, one group. We joined them for two days, but then we were alone again.
[Because you were quicker than the group?]
Both of us has been climbing up the hills, we took a shortcut to avoid the Chinese police checkpoint, but the group followed the road.
First these people helped us, so we stayed two days with them. They told us that we could sleep with them in their tent and they also gave us food. But the next day they asked us not to stay longer with them because we would be caught all together.
They told us it was better to go alone.
[Where did you sleep during the night?]
Sometimes in caves or some people let us sleep in their houses. On the way we also met three Tibetans and a foreigner who gave us a tent and some useful things to sleep.
[So you didn't have this tent from the beginning?]
No.
[Did you meet some of this group afterwards here?]
Yes, but they arrived only now; we arrived already 15 days ago.
[Why did you leave Tibet?]
We wanted to see H.H. the *Dalai Lama*.
[And what will you do after this?]
We want to become monks.
[Were you already a monk in Tibet?]
No, we were going to school; only for one year.
[Was the school far from your place?]
We had to walk for two hours to reach the school.
[And was it a Tibetan school?]
Yes, the people who are working there were mostly Tibetans, but the administration was governed by Chinese.
[Did you get Tibetan language as a subject?]
Yes.
[Do you intend to return one day?]
Now we will stay here for nine years at least to study Buddhism, after that time I would like to go and see my parents.'

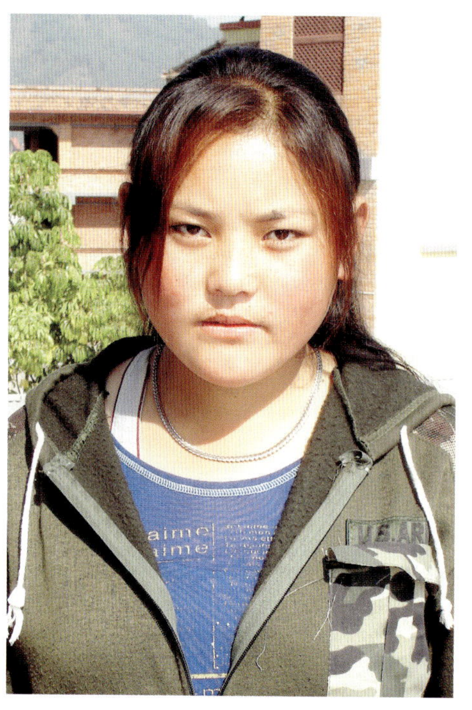

A 17 year-old from Kham was part of a large group of 108 people.

'I started travelling to Lhasa. We all gathered on a big ground and from there we left by bus. Two guides took care of us and promised us a safe delivery. I paid 3,500 *Yuan*, but some others paid 4,000. Sometimes people don't know how much they should pay because they don't have any experience. We drove all night and in the morning we had to get off the bus and climb in the mountains to hide and sleep. At night, we had to come down and we continued our trip. We did this for two nights and reached Lhatse. From there we came all the way by foot; it took us 18 days to the Nepalese border. One person got ill; he had stomach problems and frostbite. We stopped for two days, but then the guide decided to leave him behind. From the border again we took a bus but we didn't have to hide anymore.'
She came to study.

Many children have to walk for days, weeks or sometimes more than a month to reach Kathmandu. Lots of them get painful feet and legs, sometimes frostbite. Most of the time they cannot follow the normal road out of fear of being caught by the police. They have to cross forests, rivers and bridges, mostly during the night.

Two children from Kham met each other in Lhasa. The girl stayed there for several months searching for a guide, while the boy reached Lhasa with his relatives and fortunately they quickly met a guide. They reached Dram by bus in 24 hours and stayed there for two days to rest. Then they left for Kathmandu through the forest. It took them 12 days by foot; they only walked during the night. The oldest of their group was 20 years old, the youngest only seven.

'I arrived 12 days ago with a group of 30 young people and one guide. Nobody in the group had major problems, we all managed it well. We had to walk for 15 days and on the way we felt very cold. Because we were scared of being caught by the police, we walked during the night but it was so cold.'
When I asked him if he had been to school in Tibet, he said: 'Yes, I went to school for four years, but I lived a spoiled life with drinking beer, playing snooker and cards. Now I really want to study hard and learn English.'

His 20 year-old friend wants to become a monk.

'In Tibet I went to school, but the level of education was not so high. I felt I had to become a monk, so I came here.'

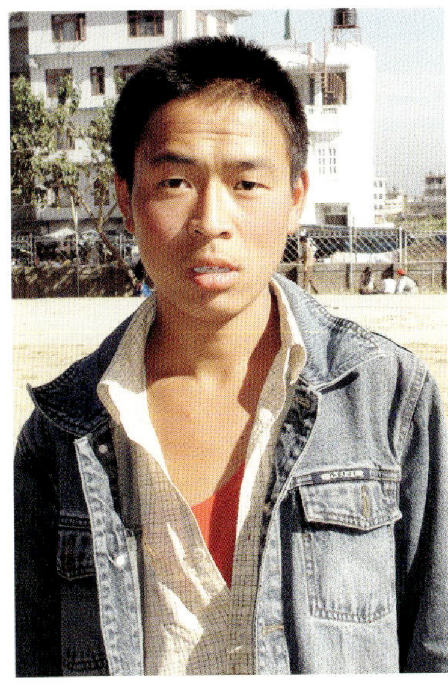

'I arrived on 13 September and I am still stuck here [on 28 November] and I even don't know when I will go to India. It took me one month and ten days to reach here. I had problems with my feet because of the cold snow. But when I arrived here, I didn't know there was a hospital, so it slowly cured by itself. I am a monk and I want to study Buddhism in the Drepung monastery in Mundgod [southern India]. Back in Tibet it was not possible anymore, but in India I will study Buddhist philosophy and become a good monk.'

When I asked him how he spends his days, he answered: 'I pray, I write, I sleep and I try not to get bored during this long waiting time. It's a really good lesson in patience.'

Waiting for the bus to go...

Many of them meet Maoists or police near the border; sometimes they just ask for money and release them immediately or after one or two days, sometimes they cause more troubles: some refugees are locked up; their clothes are stolen, etc.

'I came with a group of 26, all children between eight and ten years old. Each of us had to pay 3,000 *Yuan* to the guide. From Lhasa we walked to Mount Kailash for 12 days, from there it took us another month. Some children were a little ill; we all had wounded feet, but no frostbite. In Nepal we were stopped by Nepalese terrorists for two days and they demanded 1,000 *Rupees* from each of us. They were armed, but didn't do anything to us.'

A 14 year-old girl from Kham was very shy and did not want me to take her picture.

'I arrived here a week ago. On the way nothing serious happened. We were only three: me, a very old *amala* and one guide to escort us. Up to the border we travelled in a vehicle. Then we had to walk for seven or eight days. On the way we met some policemen and they asked me for what reason I came here. I told them I came to take a dip in the hot spring.[11] Then they asked for money, but there was a monk and he paid the police and then the problem was solved. Then I had to stay down and was covered by blankets, so that the police did not see me.'

When I ask her how she could hide under blankets while walking, she seemed to become confused. She then contradicted herself:
'I walked from Lhasa to the border and then from the border I came in a jeep. I met the police near the border.' Seeing she looks very puzzled, I do not insist. Is she going to study? 'Yes. Please, no picture'.

[11] This hot spring is located in the village Tatopani, which means 'hot water' in Nepali.

When I first asked for an interview, they were a little reluctant; but when I told them about this book, they accepted willingly. The girl, 19 years old, was about four months pregnant when she left Tibet, her husband was 21.

[You already told me you lived in Lhasa before you left.]
'We are both from different places. We met in Lhasa, I was a school student and she was working as a dancer in a hotel.
Yes, during the day I learned how to perform Indian dances, in the evening I went to the hotel to dance. I did this for four years. He came to Lhasa to do a school test.
[What kind of test?]
I went to school in Ngari up to class six and I got third position for the examinations. Then I came to Lhasa to do the test. Then I met her.
[Why did you leave Lhasa?]
After three months, we went to his place and stayed with his parents for more than one year.
[When you left Lhasa, was this because your test was not good?]
No, my test was very good, I got second position, but I wanted to become a driver. Then after one year, I wanted to come to India to study again.
But our trip was very difficult!
We really had bad luck all the time, I think I have done some bad things in the past, my karma[12] you know ... We started our journey in the evening; the whole night we climbed one hill and in the morning we reached the top. Then we went down again and we arrived in Limi. There for the first time we met Maoists. They locked us up in a room with cow dung and grass for eight days. We got food but it was not very tasty, so we threw the remaining food in the shit. Then we received no food for three days, so we started eating this food mixed with shit. Finally after three days they gave us better food.
[What did they want from you?]
There was an older man and I begged him to release us. Finally they released us. They didn't want money, but they were just looking for good clothes and took all our clothes.
After this again we walked one day and one night, and again we met Maoists, but these weren't bad. They were drinking and dancing, enjoying all together. They kept us three days but they gave us *dal bhat*. Then we continued for four and a half days, in fact we walked all the time, day and night. We met some people who spoke Tibetan and we got some *tsampa* from them, but there were small worms inside it.
Then there was a very big river which you cannot cross but there was one iron rope and you had to pay 500 *Rupees* to cross it like a monkey hanging on your hands

[12] Buddhists strongly believe that what happens to them in this life is linked with what they have done in the previous one. Negative and positive situations are the result of former actions. Therefore they think it is very important to live a good life, so that you take benefit of it afterwards.

and feet. You had to be very careful not to fall into the river and then we reached the Indian border.
[The Indian border?]
Yes, we were too far! We had been walking to the south of Nepal and we had reached the border; but we didn't know which road we had to follow, so we kept on walking and finally we reached the Indian border. There was a good road, but we were afraid of being caught and so we crossed a hill; it took us six and a half days. The road was very difficult: there was only a simple track, on one side there was this hill, the other side was very steep.
We heard about an old man and his daughter who died there. They were Khampas.[13]
I slipped but I was lucky because my shirt caught on a tree and so I was saved. Then it was already three weeks since we had left and again we met a good road, again we were afraid to go this way, so it took us three days to cross a hill, and lastly we reached Dargula in India.
My hands and legs were so swollen at the end.
[And what about the food?]
Yes, we had no good food.
From Dargula we took a bus to Delhi, it took us three days. A Tibetan woman warned us: 'If you speak, then they will know you are refugees and you will be caught.' So we didn't talk for three days, not a single word. We even tried to control our breath and made ourselves very small.
And then again when we were in Delhi, we were sleeping and suddenly everybody was running.
[Oh yes, there was an earthquake!][14]
In Delhi in the reception centre they told us to come here [to Kathmandu] to do the registration papers.
[My translator explains that they cannot do this in India, since the *UNHCR* office is here in Nepal. Sometimes refugees take the wrong road and arrive at the Indian border and then in Delhi, but they have to register in Kathmandu first.]
[When did you arrive here?]
On 10 October, so we travelled for a month. And the bad luck continues. Normally we had to leave for Dharamsala last week, but this bus didn't go.[15] I called my parents and they told us to come home.
[When is the baby due?]
In January, so we really should go now, because otherwise the journey might become too difficult.'[16]

The baby was born in Nepal in February and the young parents were forced to stay for two more months.

---

[13] Khampa, plural Khampas: inhabitant of Kham region.
[14] The Kashmir earthquake on 8 October was a major seismic event of the Himalayas, recording a magnitude of 7.6 on the Richter scale. The tremors were felt up to 1,000 km from the epicentre, so also in Delhi.
[15] From November 2005 the Nepalese government, without giving any explanation, stopped issuing exit permits to Tibetan refugees. See chapters 6 and 7.
[16] The journey from Kathmandu to Dharamsala (India) consists of a two days' travel by bus to Delhi and from there another 12-hour drive to Dharamsala.

Another gripping story is that of a 16 year-old girl from Amdo. I met her in Delhi in January 2006.

'I was the youngest; I have one brother and three sisters. Since I was born, my mother had a poor health and she was very sick. My father had a small business, but it went down and our family had a financial crisis. So they could not afford to keep me and I was adopted by another family. I was about four years old when this happened. That other family, they were nomads and lived one day away by jeep from my own home. I had to work very hard with them and I never went to school.
In 2003, I was 13 years old, my mother passed away. I heard that my mother had had a very hard time. When I was born, my father was having an affair with another woman, so there was a lot of tension and it affected her health. Afterwards my father remarried with that other woman. The family that adopted me didn't treat me so good. Especially when someone dear or near passes away, the environment should be more peaceful, people must not enjoy, but what I noticed, was that they didn't care much about me, they sometimes even scold me. I only had a good relation with their son. One of his friends lived in Lhasa and was a driver, so I was able to go to Lhasa with him and from Lhasa we drove to Dram. My stepbrother didn't know anything of my plan. At the border my friend handed me over to a Tibetan and I stayed two days with him. One Nepalese came to the place where I was staying, and I had to pay 1,000 *Yuan*. From Lhasa to Dram I didn't have to pay because it was a friend, but this Nepalese asked me for money. When it was dark, we started walking, together with two other Tibetans, a young monk and an older one. Then we drove a little bit by jeep and again we had to walk. One night we hid in a cave in the forest. These Nepalese told us they were going to look for food but they didn't come back. Luckily, I had some Tibetan cookies and the two others some dried meat, so we shared. After two days the Nepalese came back and we continued. Then we arrived in another place and that was a completely remote one, so there was also no food. I don't know exactly where we were, but there was nobody. Again the Nepalese said they would try to get some food, but they didn't. When I felt thirsty, I broke some ice and ate it; it gave me big stomach pain. In the evening we rested and in the morning we started walking again and finally we reached a village with many people and again our guides went to search for food, but now we got *dal bhat*. Then they changed our clothes, because we still had our warm clothes; I got a Nepalese dress and the monks a T-shirt and trousers. In this place we stayed for three days. One day when it was dark other Nepalese came and they asked for money. I had 500 Nepalese *Rupees* and the monks they had 2,000 *Yuan* but I didn't know how much to give, so I gave them 500. These new Nepalese were three young men, and they said you go with him, you with him and you with him and they took our bag and we went by bus. We reached a little town and entered into a big house. I thought that we were going to stay for the night, but suddenly at midnight one of them told me to go and he wanted to take me with him. I was very nervous because the two monks were not there and I shouted very loud. I saw that the two other monks were in another house and I said: 'I don't want to go, we stay together.' Then they put us together in a very dark place for ten days and we were not allowed to go out. We used the darkest corner of the room as a toilet. The Nepalese gave us food, but they asked for money for it. Since we said we didn't have any money, they took the watch of one monk, a quite expensive one, in exchange

The girl upon arrival in Nepal.
Spring 2003

for food. One Nepalese who spoke a little Tibetan, asked for 3,000 *Rupees* for each of us. 'If you pay these 3,000 *Rupees*, we will bring you to the nelengkhang [the Tibetan word for reception centre, *TRRC*]. Maybe we can take the elder monk there and then we get money and then we come back and take the two others,' he said. But we didn't accept. 'No, if we go, we go together.' Then one of these young men took me to another place but suddenly I thought: 'This is not good!' I tried to pull back, we had a little struggle and finally I bit his hand and could manage to come back.

Suddenly there was also a woman with a child. 'If you give us money, we will help you.' Then the younger monk said: 'Let's go' and we took our shoes and started running. The woman had the child, so she could not run after us. After a few hours we saw the three guides from two days before and they shouted: 'We will help you, we have your clothes and everything here!' But we were afraid and ran away. They chased us. At the riverside there were some other persons, and the Nepalese shouted to stop us. Then the younger monk became aggressive and he tried to throw a stone at them and then the two monks were beaten. Finally we could manage to cross the river and hide for a while. One of the monks knew a place, called Boudha,[17] so when we arrived in a village, we asked somebody the way and he showed us the direction. We reached one main road and tried to search for a truck or a bus. Finally we took a taxi with two men inside and after half an hour driving we asked to get out and they asked for money. The elder monk gave 100 *Yuan* and they didn't give back anything. Then we tried to get another vehicle but it was very difficult because they kicked us out whenever we showed the foreign currency. So we continued by foot. Then again we took a bus and when the driver asked for money, we showed the Chinese currency but he wouldn't accept it and he showed us with a sign that we will go to prison or have our neck cut, so we were very afraid and we got out immediately. Then in another bus we were sitting in separate seats and again they asked for money, but this time we talked a little bit and then he accepted it. At last we arrived in Boudha; it was already dark.

[17] Boudha = Bodhnath, 6 km from Kathmandu. It is a religious centre for Tibetans, with many monasteries and a huge *stupa* (built to house holy relics).

In Boudha we looked for a taxi to bring us to the *TRRC*. The monk had still 100 *Yuan* and he asked to change them, he received 500 Nepalese *Rupees*. When we asked the price to bring us to the *TRRC* he charged us 500 *Rupees*, we bargained to 300.[18] Then on the way we were caught by the police. 'What is your name? Where you want to go?' they asked. 'To the reception centre', we said and then the police took us with them. They put me in one room and the others in another room; later we were transferred to a big prison with a lot of foreigners.[19] A Tibetan woman asked me what had happened and I told her I was from Tibet. She told me not to worry because somebody from the *TRRC* would come. Indeed one Tibetan came and asked me information about the taxi driver, if I remembered the number of the taxi and he gave me 50 *Rupees*. The next day they brought me to another place. The police tried to interrogate me, but I couldn't answer because I didn't understand their language. Then they asked me for money. I thought if I give the 50 *Rupees*, maybe he will release me. But instead, I was locked up again.[20] I didn't receive any food and there was no toilet. There was also a very rude woman and I was afraid she would beat me. Again I was transferred to another place. Since I saw some Tibetans there I thought it was the *TRRC*, but it was the main prison! There was a fight between some of the prisoners and I was scared, but this staff member from *TRRC* comforted me, he said they wouldn't hurt me or send me back! In this prison I was locked up in one room with 10 women, mostly Nepalese of different ages; some were also very young, some even had a child. They also comforted me, gave me other clothes and helped me wash my hair. We only got two meals a day, so I felt very hungry in the beginning; afterwards I got used to it.
Finally I was released, in total I spent two months and a half in prison. In fact I escaped in October 2002 and I arrived in the *TRRC* in February 2003.
While I was imprisoned I was praying that no one may have this same experience, especially I was thinking of the *Panchen Lama* who has remained in prison for the last 10 years. Some refugees are really lucky to arrive easily, I had a tough time and then I got sick afterwards: TB diagnosis. But the saddest of all is that they took all the pictures of my family and of my best friend.'

Some other youngsters had a bad time. When I was interviewing Mr Lhoudup Dorjee, Director of the *TRRC*, I heard about a group of 18 refugees aged between 16 and 30 who had been caught by the police on 28 November. They were caught on the way to the *TRRC* and put in prison. Each of them faced a fine of 8,500 *Rupees* or 11 months in prison. On 4 December, the front-page of the *Himalayan*, a Nepalese newspaper, mentioned '18 Tibetans arrested... Despite attempts of the *UNHCR* and the *TRRC* to [obtain the] release [of] the refugees, the authorities did not release the Tibetans'.

After the payment of the total sum and a lot of paperwork the youngsters were finally released after 11 days.

Three of them were willing to tell me about their journey.

---

[18] The price for tourists for this distance is about 100 *Rupees*.

[19] In Kathmandu there are two main prisons: Hanuman Dhoka prison and Dill Bazaar.

[20] = Immigration Detention Centre in Kathmandu.

'In our group we were 18, nearly all from Amdo except some from Shigatse and two from Lhasa who joined us at the border. We drove one day and one night in a car from Lhasa to the border; then we walked to reach Lukla (Nepal). Sometimes we even had to cross the snow. On the way some were ill or had problems in their legs from walking. In Lukla we tried to phone to the *TRRC*, therefore we had to walk down one day, and one day up to come back. The staff from the *TRRC* told us to look for other Tibetans and so these two from Lhasa joined us. Then the police caught first two of us, then later the whole group. They took a mobile phone, 1,000 *Yuan* and a camera. Me and my friend we were thrown in prison for two days. The policeman let us go but told us: "Go back to Tibet. Just get out!" Then we ran away and we looked for the rest of the group. They stayed in the house of a *Sherpas* family. One foreigner had given money to the *Sherpa* for their food. Afterwards he denied he had received 4,000 *Rupees*, but said he got only 300 *Rupees*, just enough for tea and boiled potatoes. One day I saw the *Sherpa* writing down 100 *Rupees* for one lunch for one person. I asked him why he was writing this. He said: "No worry, these 100 *Rupees* will be given by the *TRRC*,[21] no worry." I said to him: "That is not fair because when we had food, it was never for 100 *Rupees* and the money from the reception centre is His Holiness' money."[22] Then the *Sherpa* tore up the notes, and we didn't want to stay longer. We called again the *TRRC*. Now they told us we could come down through Katari. Everybody was worrying about the fact our money would be finished before somebody would come to get us and that we wouldn't have anything to eat ... so we had a lot of thinking and tension. What to do? Then we reached the Thupten Choeling monastery.[23] The Lama of this monastery is a very good friend of H.H. and he always helps refugees. We stayed there for one night, we had dinner and breakfast. From there we walked for three days and finally we reached Katari. There we caught a bus. Since the road was not so good we had three different buses and lastly we reached Kathmandu. Near to the *stupa* of Swayambhunath[24] we were caught by the police. We were all sitting in the back of a microbus, in the front there were Nepali. A policeman came inside and took us immediately to the *Department of Immigration* (*DOI*). We stayed there for one night. In the morning the staff from TCCR came to see us and afterwards they put us in prison. It was a big prison with 900 Nepali prisoners. We remained for 11 days and we got several visitors: *Tibetan Woman Association (TWA)*, Amdo Association, and some persons of *ICT*. They told us someone was going to pay our fines and we would be released quickly.'

The ani (nun) who had not yet spoken during the whole interview told me her greatest fear was to be returned to Tibet. She wanted to meet the *Dalai Lama* and now she was going to get the opportunity.

---

21 Douglas DiSalvo (UNHCR Nepal) confirmed that local people (who may be Nepali Sherpas, or Tibetan refugees) are reimbursed for food or accommodation supplied to Tibetan new arrivals.

22 The refugee thought the Dalai Lama paid for the expenses of the *TRRC*; in fact the UNHCR finances all their expenses (see chapter 7).

23 Monastery on the trail between Lukla and Jiri. I had intended to visit this place, thinking I could get interesting information there, but the inflammable situation in Nepal, with bomb blasts every day, prevented me from attempting the trip.

24 Swayambunath is located on the outskirts of Kathmandu. On the top of a hill stands a Buddhist temple and a *stupa*.

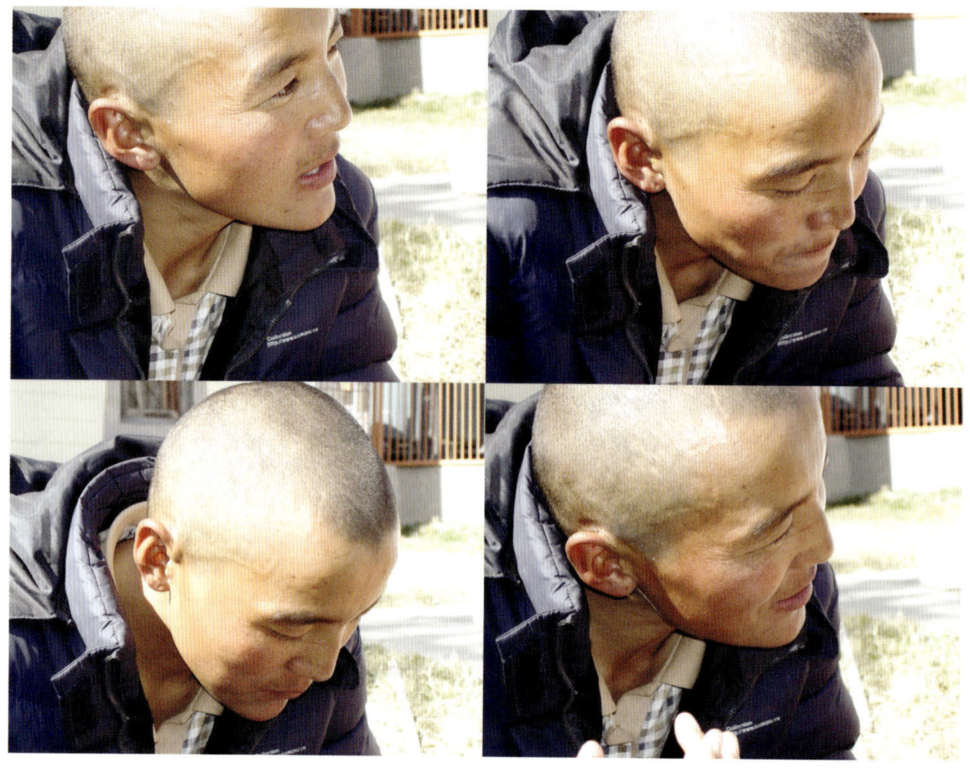

Reflecting after release

One of them concluded with this statement:

'The world should know about the problems the Nepali cause to Tibetans on their way to freedom. If this will be known, then maybe the Nepali will behave a little better. If the Nepali got a little bit of a lesson, then it will be easier for those who will come from Tibet in the future.'

CHAPTER 6

NEPAL'S ATTITUDE OVER THE YEARS (1960 to the present)

'All the organs of the state
must remain alert in honouring and upholding human rights.'
(King Gyanendra of Nepal)

Over the years Nepal's attitude changed. From 1959 to 1989 they gave shelter and provided papers for some of the refugees who had no legal status, although they had limited political and economic rights. Under the pressure of China the Nepalese government proceeded to forcible repatriation to the border, to handing over to the Chinese police; rapes, beatings and even shootings have also been reported. In 2005 they closed the two Tibetan offices in Kathmandu and stopped issuing exit permits.

In the three decades (1959-1989) following the *Dalai Lama*'s flight, Nepal had an accommodating attitude towards Tibetan refugees: at least 20,000 of them found a haven in Nepal, on top of the 10,000 more who found shelter with relatives and *Sherpas;* a generous response from a country where even today 43% of the population lives on less than a dollar a day.[1] Despite not having signed the UN Convention on Refugees,[2] Nepal respected the human rights articles it contains. Douglas DiSalvo (*UNHCR* Nepal) states: 'In Asia few countries have signed the Convention, although the UN encouraged them to do so. They follow more their own political agenda. If leader India decided to sign, maybe other countries would follow. Now it is seen as a hostile act against your neighbour that can harm your mutual relationship.'[3]

Tibetans had the right to remain in Nepal. They had limited political and economic rights, but no legal status.

Until the early seventies Nepal even tolerated the presence on its territory of members of the armed resistance to the Chinese invaders. Khampas,[4] Tibetan freedom fighters supported by the CIA,[5] operated from Mustang, a border region. At that time Communism was indeed a common enemy. But President Nixon's visit to China in 1972 ended all this and the Khampas were forced to surrender their arms to the Nepalese army.[6]

In 1974, 15,000 Tibetans were finally registered by the Nepalese government, which, however, then discontinued issuing identity cards for the next twenty years. In 1989 a huge influx of new refugees arrived from Tibet because of the precarious situation in their country (see chapter 2). Not only in Tibet, but worldwide a battle for freedom and peace took place: 1989 was the year of the fall of the Berlin Wall, the student demonstration on Tiananmen Square and its cruel repression, and the awarding of the Nobel Peace Prize to the *Dalai Lama*. Following these events, western countries and the *Dalai Lama*'s representative in Nepal put pressure on Nepal to find an agreement with the *UNHCR* for the newly arriving refugees. This so-called 'gentlemen's agree-

[1] *Dangerous Crossing,* 2001, pp. 14-15.
[2] The 1951 UN Convention Related to the Status of Refugees was an attempt to regulate the chaotic displacement of peoples in Europe after World War II. It was signed by 124 countries, but not by Nepal or India. The complete text of this convention is available online at <http://www.unhcr.org>.
[3] Interview with Douglas DiSalvo, March 2006.
[4] Khampas are natives of the Kham region. They are known for their bravery and are fierce warriors. They also accompanied the Dalai Lama on his flight to India.
[5] Further details about the armed resistance can be found in John Kenneth KNAUS, *Orphans of the Cold War* (New York, 1999).
[6] *Dangerous Crossing*, 2001, p. 16.

ment' does not allow refugees to settle in Nepal, but helps them transit through Nepal on their way to India. It is a verbal understanding between the *UNHCR* and the *DOI* operating under the Ministry of Home Affairs. The refugees are arrested by the police in the border areas, and brought either in police vehicles or by local bus to the *DOI* in Kathmandu. About half of all the escapees are processed in this way. The *UNHCR* reimburses the police for all the expenses incurred. Then the refugees are detained for two or three days by *DOI*, that notifies the *UNHCR* or *Tibetan Refugee Welfare Office (TRWO)* of their arrival. Finally they are released from detention to the *UNHCR* (see chapter 7). To ensure smooth co-operation, *UNHCR* workers started visiting the border area to inform the police about the contents of this agreement.[7]

In 1991, however, Nepal adopted a new immigration law, article 3 of which states: *'No foreigner is allowed to enter or stay in the Kingdom of Nepal without a visa.'* This article turned Tibetan refugees into illegal immigrants and provided the legal basis for deportation.[8] Even though Nepal is not a party to the Convention on Refugees, it should respect the well-established international principle preventing forced repatriation: *'No refugee shall be expelled or returned ("refouler") in any manner whatsoever ...'*.[9] [10] Although not bound by treaty to the Convention on Refugees, Nepal is not only a party to the CRC *which obliges States to ensure that a child who is seeking refugee status receives appropriate protection,*[11] but also to the Convention against Torture and Other Cruel, Inhuman or Degrading Treatment or Punishment which prohibits the return of anyone to a country where they are at risk of torture.[12]

That is why these cases of deportations are a worrying change from the Nepalese government's formerly generous attitude towards Tibetans. Although the robbing, beating, abuse and deportation of refugees have been reported, the unwritten agreement functioned quite well during the 1990s.

In 1999 Nepal was forced by international pressure to resume the registration of Tibetans. Those who arrived before 31 December 1989 together with their children are allowed to remain in Nepal, in accordance with the 'gentlemen's agreement'.

---

[7] *Dangerous Crossing,* 2001, pp. 18-21.

[8] *Dangerous Crossing,* 2001, p 18.

[9] Article 33 of the UN 1951 Convention: 'No Contracting State shall expel or return ("refouler") a refugee in any manner whatsoever to the frontiers of territories where his life or freedom could be threatened on account of his race, religion, nationality, membership of a particular social group or political opinion.'

[10] The French term "refouler" was added to the English text of the Convention to specify the exact legal breadth of the vaguer English term "return" as something roughly equivalent to "forced repatriation". On the contested legal bearing of this, see the 1993 finding of the US Supreme Court in the case of Sale v. Haitian Centers Council, on the forced repatriation of Haitian refugees intercepted by the US coastguard outside US waters, and the dissenting opinion of Justice Blackmun.
See <http://supreme.justia.com/us/509/155/index.html>.

[11] Article 22.1 of the CRC: 'States Parties shall take appropriate measures to ensure that a child who is seeking refugee status or who is considered a refugee in accordance with applicable international or domestic law and procedures shall, whether unaccompanied or accompanied by his or her parents or by any other person, receive appropriate protection and humanitarian assistance (...)'.

[12] Article 3.1 of the Convention against Torture, and Other Cruel, Inhuman or Degrading Treatment or Punishment: 'No State Party shall expel, return ("refouler") or extradite a person to another State where there are substantial grounds for believing that he would be in danger of being subjected to torture.'

These refugees are eligible to receive a Refugee Identity Card (RC). Although RCs do not provide them the same civil and legal rights as Nepalese citizens, they do confer certain civil rights and the freedom of movement within Nepal and, most significantly, security against forcible repatriation.[13]

At the same time, China increased its influence in Nepal. Over the years China's financial aid to Nepal has grown systematically. In 2005 China's $11,482,375 of development aid to Nepal was more than doubled by the additional grant of $12.3 million:[14] a huge amount for such a poor country. To maintain its friendly relations with China, Nepal adapted its attitude towards Tibetan refugees. Arrests and deportations of newly arrived refugees from Tibet, even including children, became more frequent. They are systematically not turned over to the *UNHCR*, as they had been in the past, but are tried on immigration violations and fined or sentenced to terms in prison.[15] Moreover *UNHCR* workers were no longer given permission to travel to the border to monitor the situation of arriving refugees in these areas, and the agreement was no longer communicated to the border police nor supported by the Home Ministry and the *DOI*.[16]

In the meantime, the internal political situation in Nepal became very problematic. In June 2001 most of the royal family was murdered, and a wave of Maoist violence hit the country. The police became reluctant to escort refugees to Kathmandu, and adopted a policy of deporting any Tibetan without valid travel documents.[17] At least 2,500 Tibetans were arrested on the Tibet/Nepal border. Youdon Aukatsang *(TCHRD)* described the situation: 'To leave Tibet, refugees face a dangerous journey across the Himalayas into Nepal. To then deport them back to Tibet where they will face arrest, imprisonment and torture, or to imprison them in Nepal causes even further trauma'.[18]

At the end of the year 2001 a state of emergency was proclaimed in Nepal. The Chinese government took advantage of this political instability to increase its pressure on Nepal. One result was the issuing of an order restricting Tibetan cultural and religious activities in Nepal. 'Nepalese government officials have admitted that these curtailments happen because public activities jeopardize Nepal-China relations, but that the Tibetan community was allowed to organize community events as long as they were not political activities or considered to be 'anti-China' activities.'[19]

This was accompanied by a hardening policy towards newly arriving Tibetans. As mentioned earlier, in mid April 2003, a group of 21 Tibetans was arrested, eight of them aged between fourteen and eighteen. Apart from the three smallest (two girls aged nine and six and a six year-old boy) the group was given prison sentences of up

[13] *Dangerous Crossing,* 2002 Update, p. 8; *Dangerous Crossing,* 2004, p. 4.
[14] TIN News Updates, 16 August 2005, p. 5: 'PRC pledges $ 12.3 million aid to Nepal'.
[15] *Dangerous Crossing,* 2002 Update, pp. 8-9.
[16] *Dangerous Crossing,* 2002 Update, p. 24.
[17] *Dangerous Crossing,* 2001, p. 25.
[18] TCHRD Press Release, 7 January 2002, p. 2.
[19] *Dangerous Crossing,* 2002 Update, p. 17: ICT interview with Secretary Tika Narula, Home Ministry, Kathmandu, 13 December 2002.

to ten months for entering Nepal illegally. In May they were expelled and handed over to the Chinese. It was the first time that refugees were deported from Kathmandu in a joint operation carried out by officials from Nepal and China. This took place despite widespread international concern and protest expressed by the *UNHCR*, governments and NGOs.[20] *UNHCR* stated that these individuals should be seen as 'persons of concern', but that they had been denied access to them. *UNHCR* warned that returning people before their status had been determined was in clear contravention of international law.

As a result of this "refoulement", US Senator Dianne Feinstein withdrew from the Senate a bill that would have given Nepalese textiles duty-free and quota-free access to US markets for two years. She wrote to the Nepalese government that her decision was directly linked to this "refoulement". In his reply the Minister of Foreign Affairs of Nepal stated a new policy of protection for the refugees which included a commitment that the Nepalese government will respect the fundamental international legal principle of non-refoulement and will not forcibly repatriate refugees. The policy also highlighted Nepal's intention to allow the *UNHCR* to operate without interference from the government.[21] It is regrettable, however, that this policy has as yet still not been put into practice. Deportations and various forms of harassment of refugees continued in 2004, but due to the international media attention given to the May 2003 "refoulement", it became more difficult to obtain information from the Nepalese side. The officials flatly denied the handing over of refugees to the Chinese police; instead they affirmed heaving returned 'illegal immigrants' to China.[22]

In 2005 the situation deteriorated further. On 21 January, the Nepalese government closed down the Office of the Representative of the *Dalai Lama (Tibet Office)* and the *Tibetan Refugee Welfare Office (TRWO)* in Kathmandu, saying that this action was undertaken because they were operating without being registered and against the country's foreign policy. However, both offices had been operating for 40 years. The closure of the *TRWO* in early 2005 has complicated the work of the *UNHCR* in the *TRRC*, but *UNHCR* stated that they would continue to provide assistance to Tibetan refugees (see chapter 7).

Nepal's Minister of Foreign Affairs denied this move was made because of Chinese pressure, but many observers in Kathmandu link the closure to the Chinese, since the Chinese Embassy often expressed its disapproval of Nepal tolerating an office of the *Dalai Lama* on their territory. Other observers see a link with sections of the Nepalese establishment's current dissatisfaction with the UN which, they allege, treats Nepal unfairly. On 24 January, for instance, Louise Arbour of the *UNHCR* delivered a speech in Kathmandu on the conflict in Nepal, criticizing both Maoists and the government for serious human rights violations.[23]

---

[20] Amnesty International Press Release, 2 June 2003. 'Nepal: Forcible return of Tibetans to China unacceptable'.

[21] *Dangerous Crossing,* 2004 Update, p. 16. Annex to a letter to US Senator Dianne Feinstein from Madhu Raman Acharya, Foreign Secretary, Ministry of Foreign Affairs of Nepal, written on 4 August 2003.

[22] *Dangerous Crossing,* 2004 Update, p. 19.

[23] TIN News Updates, 29 January 2005, pp. 1-2: 'Future of Tibetan offices in Nepal uncertain'.

On 5 February 2005, King Gyanendra dismissed his government and assumed direct executive powers. Maoist terror and general strikes regularly paralyze the whole country. As mentioned in the interviews in the previous chapter, even many refugees encounter problems with Maoist guerrillas on their way from the border to Kathmandu. They are detained, their money, valuables and clothes are stolen, the women abused. The Nepalese police in their turn continue to return the refugees to their Chinese counterparts, in exchange for high bounties.[24] Reports of violence against and firing on unarmed refugees have emerged (as mentioned in chapter 4). A young man who came from Tibet to visit his sister in the hospital of the *TRRC* was caught on his way back at the border and beaten to death.[25]

Even when they have arrived in Kathmandu refugees still run the risk of being picked up by the police. Police checks on the road have become legion, especially since the Maoist insurgency. 'Fresh arrivals'[26] are immediately gaoled and given high fines or long prison terms, even when they are younger than eighteen (see interviews).

In November 2005 the Home Ministry stopped issuing exit permits for Tibetans. On 18 November, the last bus to India left with 50 people. More than 1,000 refugees remained stuck, in effect 'imprisoned' for several months in the *TRRC*, that only has facilities for 200 people (see chapters 7 & 8).

Last bus going to India on 18 November 2005

Nearly fifty years after the Chinese invasion of Tibet, Tibetans seem no longer to be welcome in Nepal.

---

[24] TIN News Updates, 20 December 2000, p. 3: 'Tibetans sent back across the border as pressure increases on Nepal'.

[25] Information obtained in TRRC, November 2005. His sister has not yet been informed of the young man's fate.

[26] Term used for newcomers during Kalachakra 2006.

CHAPTER 7

ROLE OF THE UNHCR & THE TIBETAN AUTHORITIES

'If refugees are the most vulnerable
group among the world's downtrodden, then
refugee children and their mothers are the most vulnerable of
the vulnerable. During flight they are often the first to die,
victims of disease and exhaustion.'
(UNCHR Magazine *Refugees* 1998, 111, p. 15)

In this chapter we will focus on the role of the different authorities involved in the process of the transit of refugees through Nepal: the *UNHCR*, the *Tibetan Refugee Welfare Office (TRWO)* and the *Tibetan Refugee Reception Centre (TRRC)*.

As mentioned in the previous chapter, following the gentlemen's agreement between the *UNHCR* and the *DOI* it was usual for refugees to be detained by the *DOI*, before being released to the *UNHCR* and brought to the *TRRC*.

Lhoudup Dorjee, Director of the *TRRC*, told me: 'The purpose of this centre is to transit people because whoever comes here, he is not allowed to stay in Nepal. We use the word "reception", because we receive them and we send them; the function is transit facilities for the Tibetan people. This centre only exists in its current form since 1994.

The Reception Centre in Kathmandu.

Until 1979 the border was completely closed, so nobody could come out of Tibet. Then in 1979 the Chinese relaxed their policy and the people could travel to see their relatives or even go into exile. Since 1980 reception activity in Nepal has taken place from the *Tibet Office*. At that time, the number of refugees was low, like 50 to 100 a year. When refugees came into Nepal, the Tibetan community here knew the problems they were facing: they don't speak the language and they don't know the route to go to India. Initially the Tibetan community in Kathmandu started helping them through a private fund. They gave them food, assisted those who were sick or needed to go to the hospital for treatment. Then slowly the numbers increased, from 100 to 200 to 300, and after five or six years it became too difficult for the Tibetan community to manage. Then the *Tibet Office* took the initiative to find some donors to provide funds for the cost of living, the travel to India, and all these things. In 1991 the *UNHCR* office was opened because of the problem of the Bhutanese refugees and *UNHCR* also started helping Tibetan refugees from that time. In 1994 the Tibetan community of Kathmandu bought this land. The building was financed by the EU and the clinic was funded later by the American Himalayan Foundation.'[1]

While this centre is totally funded by *UNHCR*, for years the management has been provided by the *TRWO*. After its closure at the end of January 2005, the *TRWO* applied to the District Office of Kathmandu to register a new *NGO* called 'Tibetan Welfare Society'. Nine Tibetans with Nepalese citizenship were put forward to constitute the board of the *NGO* under Nepalese law. The request was referred to the Ministry of Home Affairs but has never been approved. On 31 October 2005 the *Lutheran World Federation (LWF)*, an international humanitarian organization, took over the operations of *TRWO* while the same Tibetan staff are still employed. The tasks of this new partner of *UNHCR* are providing logistics and transportation for the refugees, domestic needs and household support, health and nutrition, shelter and other infrastructure for the new arrivals.[2]

In *TRRC* refugees receive food, shelter, new clothes and shoes, and even medical assistance. Every Wednesday a Tibetan doctor comes and the clinic of the centre has its own staff of three health workers. Before they go to India all children are vaccinated against TB, tetanus, polio (children below ten); all of them get some medicine: tablets against worms, against travel sickness, and paracetamol. Victims of frostbite are treated here, while the 'heavy cases' are transferred to an outside hospital for amputation. Long term treatment is done by the Department of Health in Dharamsala.

Upon arrival refugees are registered by the staff. The registration can only be done in Kathmandu since the office of *UNHCR* is located there. Refugees who arrive by mistake in India without transiting through Nepal are sent back (as happened to some of the interviewees). On 16 November 2005 there were 725 refugees in the *TRRC;* on 2 December their number had increased to 950, due to the refusal of the Nepalese government to issue exit permits.[3] On 20 December I was told their number had reached 1,200.[4]

Upon arrival at the centre, a refugee's name, age, place of birth and other personal data are recorded. An interview takes place to check that they really come from Tibet. Since Tibetan schools in India have a good reputation, Tibetans or even Nepalese from the border region of Nepal try to get their children admitted to one of the *Ti-*

[1] Interview in TRRC, 2 December 2005.
[2] Information received from Mr Lhoudup Dorjee, Director of TRRC Kathmandu & ICT.
[3] Information received in TRRC Kathmandu.
[4] Information received from Mr Dorjee, Director of TRRC Dharamsala.

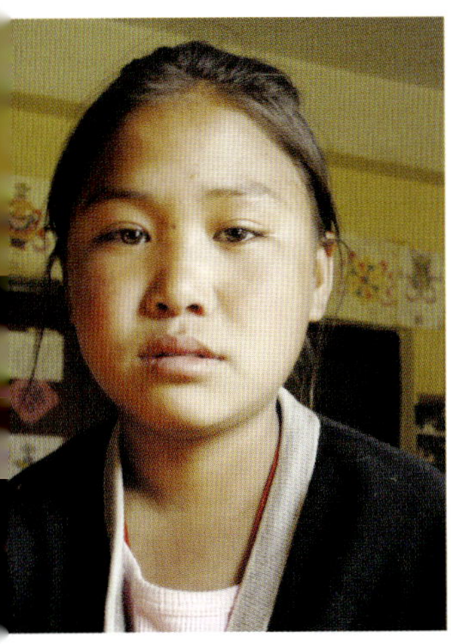

A 12 year-old Nepalese girl 'smuggled' into TRRC.

betan Children's Villages (TCV) (see chapter 9). I was told such a story: On a very busy day in November a woman from Ngari (western Tibet) brought four children between five and twelve to the *TRRC*; the staff only noticed later they were Nepalese. This woman, already known to the staff, took advantage of the crowd that day to drop the children. She recruits children from the border area and 'smuggles' them into the *TRRC*. Once they are admitted to a school in India, she returns to the parents with the enrolment number and demands 'big money', up to 100,000 *Rupees*. During the interview by the *TRRC* staff the children made a poor showing; their story was full of contradictions when they had to say which village they came from, and people from that same village did not recognize them.[5]

After the interview the refugee is given a registration card. Then they are interviewed by the officials of the Tibetan government-in-exile which categorizes them in terms of their age, reasons for leaving – to study (blue or green paper), to pursue a monastic calling (yellow) or to make a pilgrimage (white) – and afterwards determines what kind of assistance the *Central Tibetan Administration (CTA)* (see chapter 9) in Dharamsala will provide them.

Finally, *UNCHR* interviewers meet all asylum seekers in order to assess their reasons for leaving and to ensure that they are 'of concern to the High Commissioner'. Registration helps protect against repatriation, arbitrary arrest and detention by making people known to *UNHCR* and the host government as persons of concern.[6]

The *UNHCR* also plays an intermediate role when refugees are caught by the police and gaoled instead of being handed over to the *UNHCR*. They write a letter to the *DOI* to tell them these refugees might be of concern and ask that they be delivered to them.

If a refugee is 'of concern' the *UNHCR* will direct a letter of recommendation to the *DOI*, which will then issue an exit permit. This permit allows the refugee to travel from the *TRRC* to the Nepalese-Indian border, but provides no right of re-entry, legal status or refugee protection of any kind. It was issuing of this permit that was suspended from mid-November 2005. The 1951 UN Convention stipulates that *'contracting States will provide the refugees with identity papers and travel documents when they do not have any of their own'* (art. 27 & 28), *'and will ensure the issuance of documents and certificates as would normally be issued to aliens on their territory'* (art. 25). Unfortunately Nepal is not a party to this Convention.

---

[5] The staff of the TRRC intended to make a search for the woman, and also the parents, so that the return of the children could be organized. Until that time, the children remain in the TRRC.

[6] *UNHCR Handbook for Registration* (provisional release September 2003). Part 1: Principles and Standards, p. 6.

When I revisited the *TRRC* on 1 February 2006, 'only' about 800 refugees were left. The *UNHCR* had told them they could leave Nepal at their own risk without exit permit. Many of them used their savings (normally supposed to be used to start their new life in India) and travelled by themselves to India. Returning to *TRRC* one month later I was told that since the government effectively had withdrawn the request of *UNHCR* to issue exit permits, *UNHCR* had decided to provide assistance to those refugees who were not able to finance their journey to India.[7]

Since early 2003 India requires a 'Special Entry Permit for people of Tibetan origin' (see next page) that allows them to enter or exit India only from one place, called Sonauli/Raxaul. This permit, an eight-page document containing personal data and a picture of the refugee, has slowed down the transit of refugees through the *TRRC*. While before it took between ten days and one month, now it can take up to three months before they can leave Nepal. Since only fifteen refugees a day are interviewed by the Indian Embassy in Kathmandu, about 50 of them leave weekly for India.

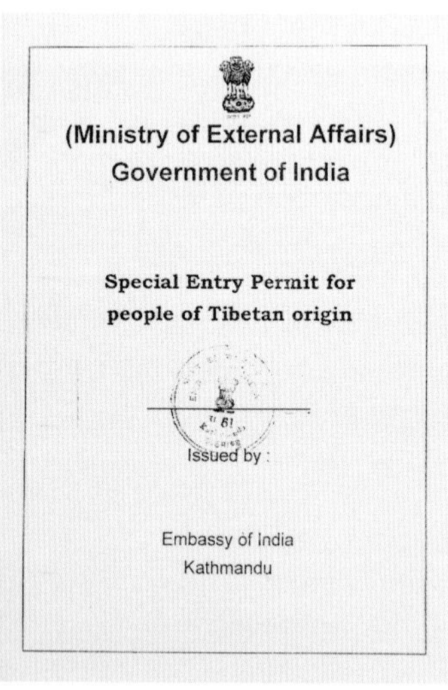
(Ministry of External Affairs)
Government of India

Special Entry Permit for people of Tibetan origin

Issued by :

Embassy of India
Kathmandu

Entry permit to India.

Two persons take it in turns to escort them to Dharamsala to ensure that everybody arrives at their destination.

'In wintertime we go once a week, sometimes two buses at a time. Now only one is going because we didn't finish all the papers. I have been doing this job for eight years. Now we have a direct bus to Delhi, before we had to change to another bus at the border. At that time we didn't have proper documents from the Indian side, so the road we used was some sort of escape road. We reached near the border, then we had to walk for 15 minutes and from there we took an Indian bus to Delhi. Normally it takes two days and two nights before we reach Delhi, it all depends on the traffic and if the weather is foggy or not. We arrive at Buddha Vihar, the office-reception centre near Interstate bus station Delhi (ISBT). If we arrive very early, then we leave the same evening to Dharamsala. Arriving after 11 a.m., we stay one day in Delhi.'[8]

The refugees carry very little with them: a *TRWO* personal identification card (as of July 2001), a daily food allowance, a health record with vaccinations received, and a record of their intended destination (i.e. coloured paper for school, monastery, pilgrimage) to be presented in the Tibetan Refugee Centre in Dharamsala.[9] The small amount of money the *UNHCR* gives to each refugee, originally meant to support them until their arrival in India, is mostly used to pay a tip to the bus driver and to the border authorities.[10]

[7] Information given by Douglas DiSalvo (UNHCR Nepal).
[8] Interview in TRRC with one of the escorts.
[9] *Dangerous Crossing,* 2001, pp. 22-23
[10] *Tibet's Stateless Nationals*, pp. 92-93

CHAPTER 8

'TRANSIT' LIFE IN NEPAL

'It is never quiet here,
during the night youngsters play outside
and in the early morning monks start their prayers.'
(Tenzin Yangkyi, health-worker TRRC Kathmandu)

What is it like to live in a reception centre? Having spent many hours in the TRRC of Kathmandu, I take you with me on a discovery tour of this place with overcrowded dormitories, the rudimentary washing facilities, and the noisy classroom with 50 children. We meet people queuing for food or registration, children waiting patiently for their vaccination injection in the clinic, some youngsters sleeping during the daytime, or frostbite patients bathing their feet. A small world without any form of comfort or entertainment.

Normally refugees spend a few weeks in Nepal after leaving for India. As we have already seen, at present their stay might last as long as a couple of months. What is it like to live in a reception centre? After entering the main gate, you have to pass through a security check. Without a permit, you are not allowed to come in. When going outside the centre the refugees have to leave their registration card at the entrance. When they want to spend the weekend with their relatives (some of them have family or friends who live in Kathmandu or in Boudha), they have to get the staff's permission and also give them their card. The relatives also hand over their ID-card to the staff: security measures to ensure that they will all return to the centre.

Once inside, a yellow building dominates the courtyard. It hosts the registration rooms (2nd floor), classroom and 3 dormitories with 30 beds each (1st floor), the kitchen and a big hall also used as a dormitory (ground floor). In total there are 200 beds, so since there were 950[1] people in residence, you saw mattresses wherever you looked: in an empty garage, on the ground-floor and first-floor terraces, in the corridor.

First-floor dormitory

[1] Number on 2 December 2005.

Some of them sleep in the corridor or outside on the terrace…

Nearly all activities take place outside.

Washing clothes or themselves.

Women's showers.

In the kitchen three cooks and seven helpers provide three meals a day. Each person has his own bowl to eat from. They queue in a long line to get their meal, then mostly sit outside on the ground to eat it. There is no dining room.

Kitchen.
Queuing for food.
Lunch.
Lunchtime.

How do they spend their days? There are no organized activities except for those in the classroom; there is no TV.[2]

Talking, praying, posing for the camera and waiting for a VIP.

[2] Some of the eating houses outside the gate have a television.

There was a basketball court, but in December a temporary tent filled the court and when I returned in March 2006 they had started a new building on that spot. Three floors with 125 bunk beds.

New building in construction.

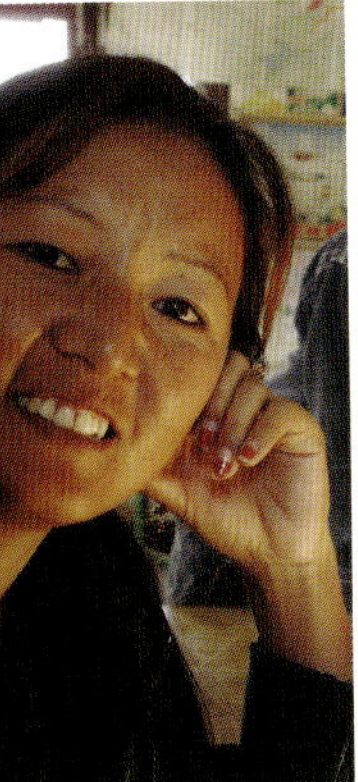

The classroom on the first floor is in use for lessons from 10 a.m. to noon, and again from 1.30 to 3.30 p.m. In the morning the two teachers, Kyi-so (see picture) and Tsering Yangchen, organize drawing, reading or other creative activities; in the afternoon children play games, make puzzles or learn the English alphabet and their first words. Children are not forced to attend class; they often run in and out while the volunteer Tibetan teacher is busy. We must not forget that most of them have never been to school so they are not used to sitting still for very long. All this happens in a relaxed, although sometimes very noisy atmosphere. This is not surprising, since most of the time between 40 and 50 children attend class (see the list of children attending class in November in chapter 2).

The only quiet place in the centre is the clinic with its small garden, an oasis of peace since only patients and their relatives are allowed to stay here. The three health workers provide first aid to those with minor diseases, such as stomach problems caused by poor food or eating snow. Children often have chickenpox or measles, their resistance reduced by the bad sanitation or the food.

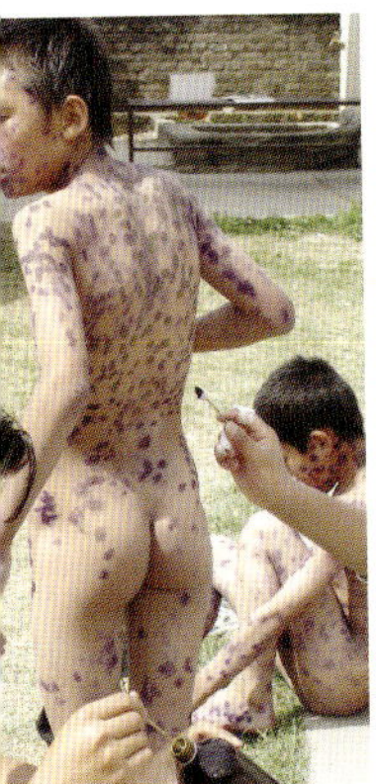

Children with measles.
Disinfection session.

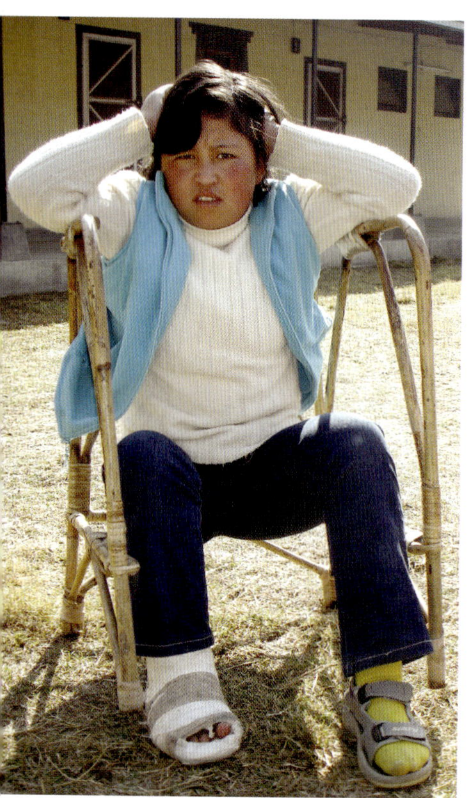

Recovering girl while relaxing

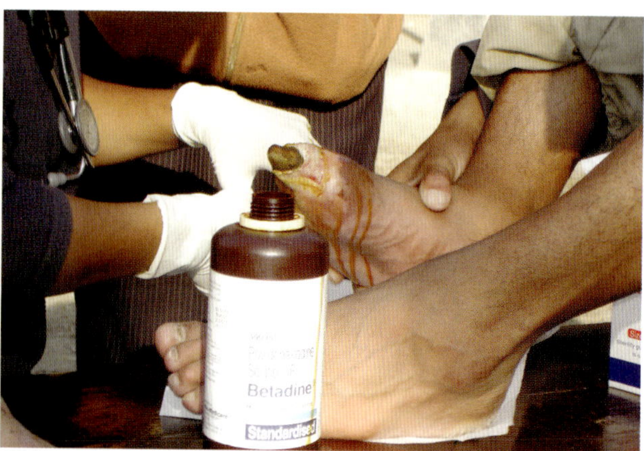

An English volunteer doctor nursing frostbitten feet

Before leaving, they are all vaccinated. Several people with lip, neck or bone problems that went untreated or were badly treated in Tibet undergo an operation or are sent to a rehabilitation centre. I met a 16 year-old girl who arrived with a foot problem and was operated on by an orthopaedic doctor. After five months in the hospital, she returned to *TRRC* where she had spent a further seven months in the clinic. She had to walk with a walking frame, but the last time I saw her, she had got crutches.

Frostbite patients have to soak their feet daily in a lukewarm bath with betadine, until their wounds are cured.

The monotony of life in the centre is only occasionally 'disturbed', by the visit of a VIP, or by a bus leaving for India, or by a bus arriving. One day, while I was conducting an interview on the steps of the main building a bus arrived through the main gate. This was one of the two groups I had been told were on their way. The guide had called the *TRRC* to tell them that there were refugees at the border, and one of the escorts went to get them. Some guides do not want to come all the way to Kathmandu and phone the *TRRC* or the *UNHCR*. The bus that arrived was a group of 42 people. They had encountered a little problem at Thangkot, a checkpoint at the entrance of the Kathmandu valley. Thanks to a UN paper they got through. I was touched by the welcome the residents of the centre gave to these newcomers. They shouted, 'Tashi delek!', 'Welcome!', and clapped their hands as if they were happy that another group had arrived safely. The other group, a group of 18 people, was less fortunate; the police caught them (see interviews).

A 'disturbance' of another kind was the crying of a new-born baby. Between November and February two mothers gave birth while staying in the centre and in March a woman arrived seven months pregnant. She gave birth two weeks later, and was still residing in the hospital during my visit.

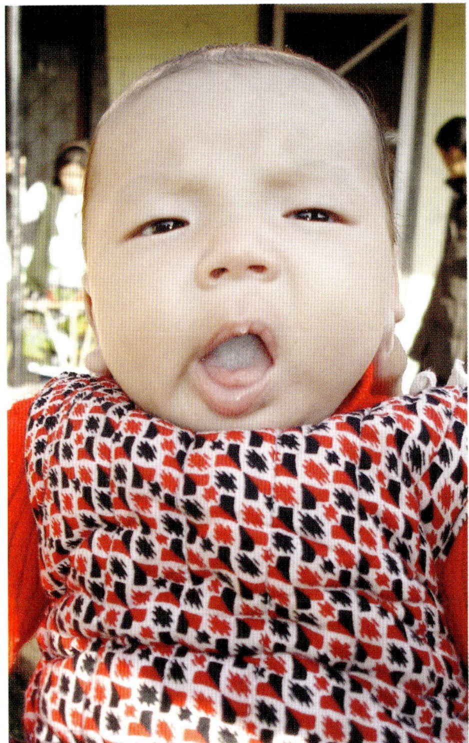

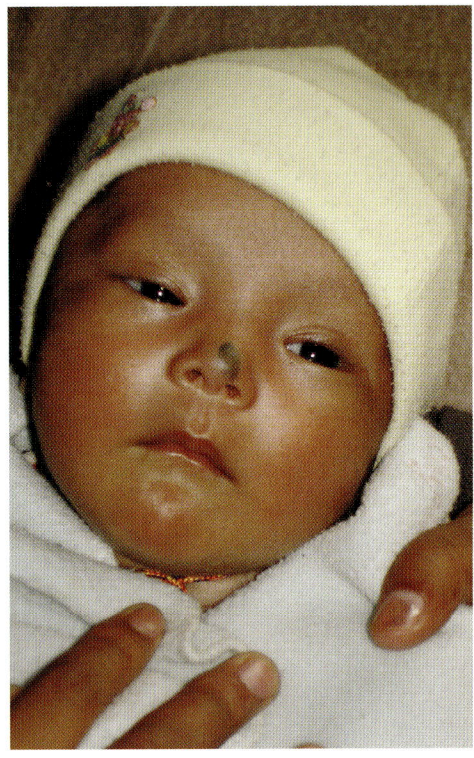

To be born in a refugee reception centre ... there are better ways to start your life.

CHAPTER 9

RECEPTION & SCHOOL FACILITIES IN INDIA

'Education for peace.
All our efforts to help children in need
are ultimately a contribution towards peace.'
(Prof. Dr H. Gmeiner)

Once they arrive in India, all refugees first go to see H.H. the Dalai Lama in Dharamsala. Then after a brief stay in the TRRC the children are dispatched to the different schools: those between 6 and 13 are sent to one of the *Tibetan Children's Villages (TCV)* or to the *Tibetan Homes Foundation (THF)* in Mussoorie; those between 14 and 17 go to the TCV Suja/Bir; and the group of young adults (18 to 30) are admitted to the Transit school in Dharamsala.

1. RECEPTION FACILITIES

After a 48-hour trip, the refugees arrive in Delhi, where they pass through the Reception Centre and have to fill in some papers again. Then they all 'go up' to see the *Dalai Lama* who resides in Dharamsala. It takes another 12-hour bus trip to reach this small hill town in Himachal Pradesh (northern India) where the *Dalai Lama* was given refuge after escaping from Tibet.[1] As mentioned before, in early 1979 there were very few refugees, and it was the security department, together with some private offices and the *Kashag*, who took care of them. There was no reception centre at that time; the refugees slept in a guesthouse or with relatives. At that time, food was not provided.

-ance of the TRRC in Dharamsala. December 2005.

From 13 June 1990, in response to the increasing number of refugees, *TRRC* opened its doors. Like in Kathmandu, food, medicines and clothes are free and paid for by *UNHCR*, several NGOs, and private donors.[2] There is room for between 175 and 200 refugees, or even as many as 250 if the terrace is used. During my visit in December 2005, the centre was nearly empty since most of the refugees were stuck in Nepal; only a few children, and two dozen elderly and sick people were in residence. On the second floor I met Ama Adhe,[3] who has worked there for 17 years as a teacher; she showed me the empty classroom and the cupboards full of toys, pencils, games, and clothing waiting for the children to come.

[1] The English administrators used to reside in Dharamsala during the summer, since the climate is cooler than in Delhi. In 1947, when India became independent, the place became a ghost town. In 1960 the Nowjorees, a wealthy and influential family, suggested to the government that Tibetan refugees be settled here. Upper Dharamsala, better known as McLeod Ganj, has become a popular tourist destination.

[2] Interview with Mr Dorjee, Director of TRRC Dharamsala, December 2005.

[3] In 1958 she was imprisoned for 27 years after taking part in underground activities. Women played indeed an important role in the resistance movement. You can read her life story in *Ama Adhe. The Voice that remembers: A Tibetan woman's inspiring story of survival* (Boston, 1997).

Classroom in TRRC Dharamsala.

'It was at the request of H.H. the *Dalai Lama* that I started working here. He asked me to teach the children the Tibetan language in a smooth way, not by shouting, because most of them had never been to school in Tibet. When they arrive, they receive a set of stationery that they can keep. In the morning they have 2 hours of drawing, in the afternoon they can play freely. I also talk with them about the fact that they have lost their freedom and then the children make drawings of their flight experience and we put them here outside on the wall. I also teach them how to wash themselves, how to put on their own clothes, how to eat properly. I am a bit like their mother and consider them as my own children. Sometimes I work alone; sometimes we are two or three teachers, Tibetans as well as volunteers. As you see everything is ready ... only the children are missing.'

During my second visit in March 2006, the centre was again filled with children and adults who had reached safety.

Upon their arrival in the *TRRC*, the children are interviewed by *CTA* officials in order to identify more permanent and appropriate arrangements. Afterwards, each of them heads for their destination: school or monastery. Children are divided according to their age: those between 6 and 13 are sent to one of the *Tibetan Children's Villages* (*TCV*) or to the *Tibetan Homes Foundation* (*THF*) in Mussoorie; those between 14 and 17 go to *TCV* Suja/Bir; and the group of young adults (18 to 30) go to the Transit school in Khanyara district in Dharamsala (see below).

Often small children are brought to Dharamsala by their parents, either both together or only one parent who returns to Tibet once their child has been admitted to one of the schools.

During *Kalachakra* in January 2006 there was a temporary reception centre to receive those refugees who come straight from Tibet without transiting through Nepal.

Entrance of the Reception Centre in Amaravati.

Security checks were carried out by Indian policemen. Photography was strictly forbidden for security reasons; many of the residents were adults returning to Tibet. People were sleeping with 15 in one large tent[4] and food was provided free of charge. A lot of them faced health problems due to the hot climate, with the temperature often about 35°C, and poor hygiene. Having no resistance to tropical diseases, they were easy victims to malaria or TB, and many suffered a variety of skin problems. All this in spite of the efforts of the local government (the state of Andhra Pradesh – South India) to provide sanitation and reduce the risk of malaria by spraying huge quantities of heavy insect repellent all over the area daily.

[4] Nearly all the participants at this gathering slept in tents.

2. LIFE & SCHOOL FACILITIES

Situation in the early years

From the beginning the refugees faced the problem of survival. The *Dalai Lama* told them they would have to stay longer in India than expected and that it would be necessary to settle mentally as well as physically.[5]

In the early sixties, the Indian government started hiring Tibetans as workers on construction sites and for building the roads in the mountains of North India. It was not only physically hard and dangerous labour, but this way of life also had a devastating effect on the family, for families had to be constantly on the move, and with both parents working all day, there was almost no supervision for small children.[6]

Children arrived in the early sixties (THF Archive)

'I was born in 1960 during the flight of my parents. While they were both working on the road, I was attached to a tree. I had a horrible childhood.'[7]

On 3 March 1960, the *Dalai Lama* opened the first Tibetan school in Mussoorie (Uttaranchal-North India). He decided to have their own schools in which the emphasis could be placed on their own culture, although a few refugee children had already started school in Indian public schools in Kalimpong (Sikkim) and Darjeeling.

'When H.H. the *Dalai Lama* came to India, he was given a residential place here in Mussoorie, the Birla house. It was here that Prime Minister Pandit Jawaharlal Nehru met him and it was also here that the Tibetan government-in-exile was first established. Later on it was moved to Dharamsala. So at that time a lot of Tibetans would come here following the *Dalai Lama*, and the need to educate the children was a priority. It was with the help of the Indian government that the first Tibetan refugee school was set up in Mussoorie; the school, which is now called Central School for Tibetans, started with 50 students. You will find such schools in most of the Tibetan settlements now and it is still supported by the Indian government.'[8]

[5] *From the Roof of the World. Refugees of Tibet* (Berkeley, Cal., 1992), p. 110.
[6] *From the Roof of the World*, p. 56.
[7] Interview with Karma Chungdak, December 2005.
[8] Interview with Mr Kelsang Namgyal, Sponsor Secretary of THF, March 2006.

On 17 May 1960, fifty-one ill and malnourished children from the road construction camps arrived in Dharamsala. Mrs. Tsering Dolma Takla, the elder sister of the *Dalai Lama*, started looking after them. The centre was called 'Nursery for Tibetan Refugee Children' (= Bhusokhang). Originally it provided only basic care and it had no school.[9] In the beginning, lack of funds, co-ordination and management skills made the situation desperate, if we can believe the diary of a volunteer from 1963:

'When we arrived at the Dispensary at 5.30 a.m., my first job was to put two children, who had died during the night, into the cardboard boxes which serve here as coffins. They were both four year-olds but malnutrition had left them as small as an average two year-old; it's quite impossible to cure such miserable scraps once they have measles, bronchitis or dysentery.'[10]

In 1964, Mrs Tsering Dolma Takla passed away and was replaced by Jetsun Pema, the younger sister of the *Dalai Lama*, who is still active today as the President of the *TCV*. Gradually the Nursery came to rely not only on the support of the Indian government but also on international aid. A massive reorganisation plan was set up since there was a huge problem of overcrowding. The *Dalai Lama* stressed the need to set up homes where the hundreds of orphans, semi-orphans and destitute children would be provided with a normal upbringing.[11] With the help of international donors the Nursery took the shape of a small village with its own school and homes.

Small children dormitory and school buildings in TCV Dharamsala

---

[9] TCV Information Brochure, p. 7.

[10] Dervla MURPHY, *Tibetan Foothold* (New Delhi, 1988), p. 28.

[11] Walter Robert Corti got the idea in 1944 to construct villages for children orphaned by the war. On 28 April 1946, the first stone of the Pestalozzi village (Trogen, Switzerland) was laid. Volunteers from different countries helped with construction and the first children were admitted and lived in family-like structures. In 1960 a first group of 20 Tibetan children arrived. See <http://www.pestalozzi.ch>.

It was in fact Heinrich Harrer[12] who asked Hermann Gmeiner, Founder of the SOS Children's Villages[13] to study the possibility of such villages for the Tibetan refugee children. In 1969 a study was carried out and in 1971 the first home was built in Dharamsala.[14] In 1972 *TCV* was fully registered and a fully fledged member of SOS Kinderdorf International. Next to *TCV* Upper Dharamsala there are now *TCV* SOS villages in Ladakh, which in the seventies was one of the most remote and least developed communities in exile and is now serving both Tibetans and Ladakhi; in Bylakuppe (southern India); since 1997 in Gopalpur (Himachal Pradesh) and also in Suja/Bir (Himachal Pradesh).

In November 1962 *THF* was born, with three homes and 75 children. Mrs Rinchen Dolma Taring (1910-2000) was called to work at the *THF* by the *Dalai Lama* and over a period of 13 years *THF* grew to 25 homes. Even though she had to resign in 1975 due to her poor health, she remained involved till her death.[15]

Group of children in the early sixties (THF Archive)

[12] H. Harrer, a famous Austrian mountaineer, died on 7 January 2006, at the age of 93. He is known worldwide for his book *Seven Years in Tibet*, which recounted his experiences in Tibet after escaping internment in British India in 1944. This book brought Tibet and its tragic situation to the attention and conscience of the world and in 1997 a Hollywood movie was based on it.

[13] The first SOS Children's Village was built in Imst (Austria) in 1949. At present there are 35 SOS Children's Villages in India, with corresponding SOS Youth Facilities and SOS Kindergartens, 15 SOS Hermann Gmeiner Schools, 9 SOS Vocational Training Centres, 4 SOS Social Centres, and 8 SOS Medical Centres. See <http://www.soschildrensvillages.org>.

[14] Sofia STRIL-REVER, *Enfants du Tibet*, p. 145.

[15] THF Information Brochure, pp. 7, 11, 12.

'And of course there were a lot of orphan children, many children lost their parents on the way. So *THF* was set up specifically for these orphan children, it did not start as a school. Family homes were set up where these orphans could be taken care of. There were foster parents who were looking after these children and gave them a normal upbringing. From Mussoorie the *Dalai Lama* shifted to Dharamsala and there again there were a lot of orphans and children to take care of, so *TCV* started with a sort of day-care centre. *TCV* started also looking after children and slowly there was more support from NGOs and individuals. We and *TCV*, we are like sister organizations; we both look after children and senior citizens. The management is separate, but we are working for the same cause.'[16]

THF and TCV: Tibetan homes system

THF homes Mussoorie

As we have said, *TCV* and *THF* both function with the homes system, the so-called Khimtsang. The children live in a home with their foster parents. Each home has a mix of younger and senior children and mostly also of boys and girls. The working of the homes is unique in itself, the day-to-day work of cooking, washing and cleaning is done by the children themselves, helped by the parents. Duty rosters are made involving all senior children, and they each get a younger child to look after: they wash their clothes, help them with bathing and with their homework. This generates a sense of belonging to a family and of responsibility.

There are two types of Family Homes: the larger ones with 30 to 40 children where a couple looks after the children, and the smaller SOS Tibetan Village homes with only 12 to 14 children looked after by a Mother.[17]

'From the beginning we were working on the same lines: looking after these children, giving them a normal Tibetan upbringing. Of course over the years, we have learned many things. Where changes were needed, we made changes. Now we have senior boys' and girls' hostels from grade X to grade XII. We cannot keep them in a family anymore, they need to live separately, need more freedom in the sense that they should not be looking after the younger children or cooking. They have to focus more on education, so they need that freedom and responsibility to live independently. The initial idea stayed the same, only minor changes have been made. Foster parents are screened before we employ them to see if they are suitable for the job. Apart from looking after the children, we give them other duties, like being a driver, or looking after a store. We also organize various workshops, especially for the mothers. We

[16] Interview with Mr Kelsang Namgyal, Sponsor Secretary of THF, March 2006.
[17] THF Information Brochure, pp. 16 & 17.

cannot run a separate workshop for every new mother that comes, but usually every year we do one, on different kinds of topics: Tibetan language, English, mathematics, classes on general cleanliness headed by the hospital section, tailoring, electricity: how it works, how to change a fuse, etc., practical classes; and then of course from the spiritual point of view again, classes by a religion teacher who would tell the mothers the religious aspect to their job, from the point of view of religion, what motherhood means and what is expected from a mother and of course our general secretary would sometimes take a few classes and talk about general topics like health, cleanliness. Apart from these, sometimes the Department of Health organizes workshops for home parents, for both father and mother, in regard of tackling psychological problems and apart from that general health topics: TB, HIV-AIDS, hepatitis, and dental care. From time to time the persons from these departments go and speak to the home parents along with the children.'[18]

Timetable

Tibetans are used to getting up early and schools are no exception to this. Children get up at 4 or 5 a.m., depending on their age. There might be minor differences from school to school, but a child's average day would look something like this:

5 a.m.	Rising bell
6 a.m.	Morning prayers and study
8 a.m.	Leave for school
8.30 a.m.	School bell and assembly
12.45 p.m.	Lunch
3.15 p.m.	School over
4 p.m.	Tea and play time
5.30 p.m.	Evening prayers
6 p.m.	Study hour
7 p.m.	Dinner
9 p.m.	Bedtime

[18] Interview with Mr Kelsang Namgyal, Sponsor Secretary of THF, March 2006.

Assembly (= morning gathering) and praying in THF Mussoorie.

Lunchtime in a TCV home

Education

In 1961, the *Dalai Lama* requested the Indian Government to establish the Tibetan Schools Society, now called the Central Tibetan Schools Administration (CTSA), to manage and assist schools in India for the education of Tibetan children.

Next to the CTSA schools there are the so-called Autonomous Body Schools, which include schools administered by the *TCV* or *THF*.[19]

In total there are now about 80 schools, with a collective total enrolment of 28,377 Tibetan students.[20]

---

[19] These Autonomous Body Schools also include the Sambotha Tibetan Schools Administration that oversees 17 schools in India and 4 in Nepal directly subject to the Department of Education, 5 schools managed by other Tibetan charitable organizations, and the 12 Snow Lion Foundation Schools in Nepal. See <http://www.tcewf.org>: Tibetan Children's Educational and Welfare Fund.

[20] Total number of Tibetan students in India, Nepal and Bhutan (April 2004-March 2005), given by the Department of Education in Dharamsala.

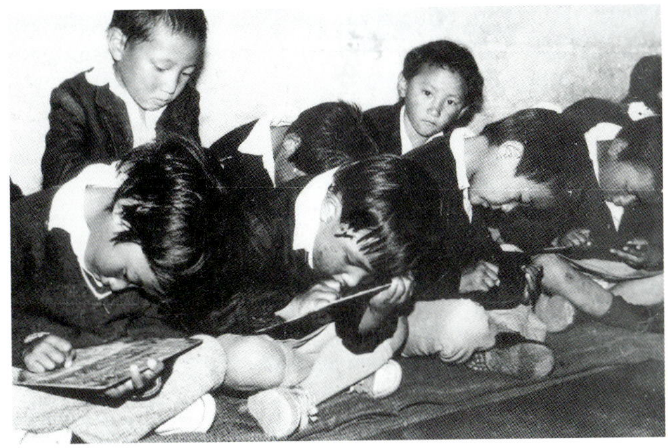

Children in the sixties in THF (THF Archive)

Children in TCV Dharamsala

'In the beginning the school followed the Indian system. From 1986 onwards Tibetan became the medium of instruction and all the books had to be translated from English. During this translation job, lots of information about Tibet was added for the Tibetan children who were born in India and had no knowledge about their homeland.'[21]

A special Education Development and Resource Centre (EDRC) produces textbooks, teaching aids, educational equipment and other resource materials. Today, all the primary schools in exile follow TCV's Tibetanization curriculum. A new education policy was approved in September 2004 and is in a test phase (see appendix 1 for the complete text of the new education policy).

---

[21] 'Tibetan children: what about their future?' Conference given by Jetsun Pema in Paris, 16 October 2003 (organized by Aide à l'Enfance tibétaine).

For the education of the young refugees an adult education centre was founded in Bir by the *Kashag* in 1986, named New Tibetan School, with 68 students. *TCV* took over responsibility for it in 1990, by which time there were already 322 students. Although *TCV* Bir is still the only place young adults are sent to, now there is a natural mix of children of all ages.

At this moment the school is bursting at the seams. There are not enough beds for all the pupils, additional mattresses are being made as a matter of urgency. The little ones already sleep two to a bed, and in some dormitories even the older girls have to share beds. Nor are there enough classrooms, three classes have lessons in the big community hall, and a dining hall is now used as a girls' dormitory.

On 21 March 2006, no fewer than 2,115 children were living there.

TCV Bir:
Assembly:
Rows of newcomers without uniform
Evening prayers

Since most of the new arrivals have never been to school , they stay for two years in an Opportunity class. In *THF* it is called Special Class. In these classes newcomers follow intensive courses of Tibetan, English and mathematics to catch up with other students, so that they can join class VI. Some of them, however, do not succeed, as mathematics is quite a tough subject for many Tibetans. In that case they shift into the section for vocational training: *thanka* painting or tailoring.

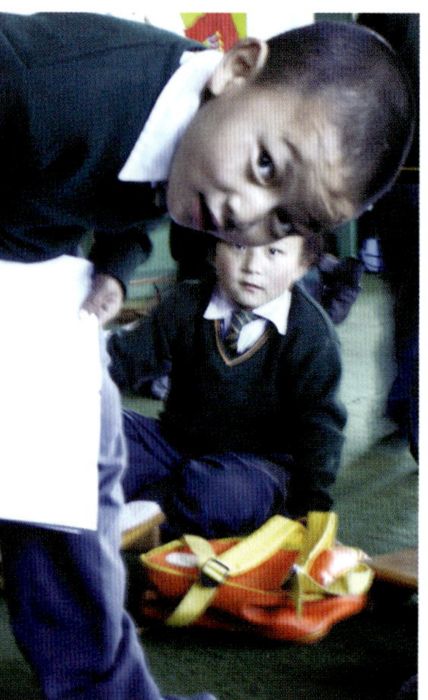

Children in THF Mussoorie

'One aspect to which a lot of stress has been given from the very start is to encourage the Tibetan arts and crafts. So at the moment we are running a vocational training centre, which was already there in the late sixties or early seventies. We have worked on most of the traditional crafts: stitching shoes, *thanka* painting, weaving carpets and aprons. We wanted to encourage that, but we also have to see the practical aspect, and we found that some crafts would not give a good career to the children. At the moment we have three different sections: *thanka* painting, modern oil painting, and a tailoring section. At first we had only Tibetan dresses, now we also have modern dresses and students have to graduate from both sections, they should know both when they start working. At the moment we have 70 to 80 children who study in these classes, and these children don't live in the family system. Since they are grown up, they live by themselves in boys' and girls' dormitories.' [22]

TCV founded vocational training centres in Dharamsala, Ladakh and Bir. A vocational and technical centre was founded in Dehradun with the objective to provide a range of technical skills (computer, mechanics, ...).

---

[22] Interview with Mr Kelsang Namgyal, Sponsor Secretary of THF, March 2006.

Boys in THF in Mussoorie (THF Archive)

Another way to promote Tibetan culture and heritage is the 'Tibet week' organized at the end of the academic session, at the end of October.

Tibet Week (THF Archive)

'This is basically because we are living in a different environment here, although we have tried to have all Tibetans together and more or less everything around is Tibetan, still in a wider area, it is a very different environment and over the years we have also been influenced by our surroundings in our food, our clothes. The Tibet week is basically held to remind our children and staff members that we all are Tibetans; we try to organize activities which remind us of our own. The first thing is that all food is Tibetan: *tsampa*, Tibetan tea, thukpa (noodle soup). The children do not wear their uniform but the traditional dresses, even we staff members in office also wear that. Apart from this, in the classes there are different activities, interclass competitions during which they are given different topics and they have to work on them. For example the *Dalai Lama*, they can give info about this, pictures etc., or the government-in-exile. There is a day that they have to explain their topic before the judges, and they are given marks and the winner receives an award. Every morning during school assembly we have certain Tibetan intellectuals, who come and speak on different topics, centring on Tibet. Classes are decorated with the portrait of the *Dalai Lama*, they put an altar and prayer flags. And in Tibet we don't have chairs, so you will see them all sitting on the ground.'[23]

All together, the *TCV* schools (including residential schools, day schools, day-care centres, vocational training and higher studies) have 16,035 students enrolled.[24]

THF has two branches, Mussoorie and Rajpur, and they take care of 2,400 children. They receive about 200 new students a year.

For the sake of completeness, we should also mention the Transit school (Sherab Gatsel Lob-ling) where refugees between the ages of 18 and 30 can go. This school, situated at the Khanyara district (Dharamsala), was established in 1992 and depended on the *TRRC*. In 2002 it was transferred to the Department of Education. At this moment 700 students reside there. For a five-year period they can study English and Tibetan, up to class VIII levels. Next to this language section there are also vocational training classes which teach *thanka* painting and tailoring. Here they do not learn languages but mathematics, useful when they start their own business.

Interview

Sunset on the Prayer Flag Hill in Mussoorie

During my visit of *THF* in Mussoorie, situated in the area called Happy Valley, I had the opportunity to interview an eleven year-old boy. The difference between him and the children I interviewed in Nepal was enormous. He was also the first child who asked me to explain how my tape recorder worked, and he wondered how I would be

[23] Interview with Mr Kelsang Namgyal, Sponsor Secretary of THF, March 2006.
[24] Number on 30 September 2005, provided by TCV Head Office in Dharamsala.

able to write down the interview if I did not know Tibetan. None of the other children had shown any interest in the tape recorder. Even during the interview he regularly checked whether it was still functioning. His way of recounting his journey was very vivid, and he made us laugh more than once.

'I was the only child in a group of 48 persons. We were walking in the snow at night, everything looked white and the snow cracked under our feet, like *crock, crock.* In some places the grass was very dry and when we walked on it, the grass pricked us and I had tears rolling down my face and I remembered my mother. (...) Then there was one place where there was security, the Chinese were there and we had to bend down and quietly slip away. [He shows me how he walked]. (...) What was very important was that we all walked together; sometimes the guide called me and told me to come back. We also crossed five bridges made out of ropes; there you had to be very careful. After that there was a wooden bridge which was quite easy to cross. (...) When I was in the *TRRC* in Kathmandu we were given food and we had to line up. If you didn't feel like eating, you could just drop it and pigeons would come and eat it. If at lunch you didn't want to eat the meat, you just threw it down and vultures would pick it up and fly away.'

When I ask him if there were many people when he was there, he replies:

'There is a ground floor and there were not many people but at the top floor there were a lot of Tibetans who used to recite prayers. The older ones recite proper prayers while we the little ones were supposed to recite 'Om mani padme hum'.[25] At night when we had to sleep, me and my three friends we quietly slipped out of the room and stayed outside. There were a lot of lights, so it was really nice to see them. As we heard the warden coming, we went quickly inside and he asked 'Where are those kids who were outside?' And we stayed still and he didn't find out.'

Of his bus journey from Kathmandu, he remembers that he left in the afternoon and that they were given a drawing book, coloured pencils and some pocket money.

'There were two buses. On the way the boy who was sitting behind me was vomiting on my clothes and I also didn't feel so good due to the road. While I was in the bus, I heard a train but I saw only half of it, I couldn't see the face. It was the first time I saw a train. On the way during the afternoon we sang and at night we slept. During the night this boy vomited and I put my hand behind me and felt a lot of it and the next morning I cleaned everything. When I arrived in Dharamsala it was raining a lot. And in the *TRRC* I broke my hand. I jumped from one bed to another, they have these bunk beds and I hit my hand on the edge of the bed and I broke my hand. In fact one of my friends pushed me and then he said sorry. I told him you don't have to say sorry, it's OK. When I broke my hand, I remembered my mum and dad. They

---

25 The most famous Tibetan mantra of Chenrezig, the Bodhisattva of Compassion. Tibetan Buddhists believe that saying this mantra, out loud or silently to oneself, invokes the powerful benevolent attention and blessings of Chenrezig, the embodiment of compassion. The mantra has several meanings; a popular translation is 'Hail the jewel in the lotus.' For an exhaustive explanation: <http://www.dharma-haven.org/tibetan/meaning-of-om-mani-padme-hung.htm>.

took me to a big hospital where they put a plaster and I had to stay there for a while. The doctor advised me not to drink sweet tea, but I did and when he asked me if I had tea, I said no.'

I ask him if he went to school in Tibet.

'Yes, I went for three years to a Chinese school in Lhasa. We were given uniforms for which we had to pay, also books we had to pay. Here we wear a tie, but there we wore a red scarf with stars [the emblem of the People's Republic of China]. The school was quite strict; we could not take any sweets into class. Every morning our pockets were checked and if they found a sweet they would take it and put it into a box. We were 25 children, only two or three were Chinese. We were taught Chinese and Tibetan and in class 5 or 6 they give computer. I was in class 3. When I was in Dharamsala, I was told that I was going to Mussoorie and since in Tibetan 'ri' means mountain, I was already imagining that it was a nice place in the mountains. When I arrived here, I really saw the mountains.'[26]

What impresses me when I visit all these different schools was the diligence of the students. At 4 a.m., at sunset or late in the evening, you could see them walking around or sitting somewhere with their books. It is clear that these children seize with both hands the opportunity for a good education and a bright future that they are offered in India.

'Children, at present you are all young
but day by day you will grow up
into good, healthy, noble and fine looking Tibetans.
I look at you with the greatest of hopes,
In future you will have to bear
the responsibilities of Tibet's religion, politics
and government and therefore you
must thoroughly know history, traditions
and language ... besides getting modern education.'

H.H. XIVth Dalai Lama

Boy studying in THF Mussoorie

Written on a panel made by students of TCV Bir.

[26] Interview March 2006.

CHAPTER 10

PSYCHOLOGICAL EFFECTS

'When I see other children,
I think I suffer a lot. I want
to play like the rest of them.'
(*A Generation in Peril*, p. 108)

Medical studies confirm that Tibetan children suffer from posttraumatic stress and more upon their arrival in India. Art therapy (poetry, drawing, ...) is an excellent manner to let children give expression to their feelings, their fear and anger. Jetsun Pema for her part prefers not to look back on suffering. My experience is that although most of the child refugees seem happy in their new environment, they all share the feeling of being a displaced person, without a country and away from their parents.

'He [a child aged 5] was very sad and quiet when he arrived here [in the reception centre]. He never played with other children, although he did come to the classroom. He never participated in any of the activities.'

'He didn't speak to anybody, he didn't eat. Only Lama Jigme managed to break through the wall of silence.'[1]

How deeply are children affected by their escape? One need not be a psychologist to know that such a journey, especially for children of young age, causes trauma and emotional stress. They sometimes suffer from anxiety, nightmares, insomnia,[2] but much depends on how tough their trip was and how strong they are themselves.

'The uprooting, disruption and insecurity inherent in refugee situations can harm children's physical, intellectual, psychological, cultural and social development. (...) During refugee situations, children face greater risks to their psychological development. Hardships in refugee situations are chronic. Children may be living in constant fear or anxiety (...) Children are affected not only by what happens to them, but by what they are deprived of, for example missing out on developmental essentials such as play and school.'[3]

Several medical studies have been conducted concerning the impact of traumatic experiences on Tibetan refugees.[4]

Refugee children in Dharamsala were examined for Posttraumatic Stress Disorder (PTSD) and Major Depressive Disorder (MDD). 'The average children's age was 12.6 years old and equally representative of males to females. There was a trend for more cases of full criteria PTSD and MDD amongst children who had recently arrived (<18 months). Children in exile suffer levels of stress-related disorders comparable with those of children in war situations or those exposed to natural disasters. However, in this population, several protective factors may help reduce the level of distress over time.'[5]

---

[1] Information given by H.V.

[2] *A Generation in Peril*, p. 108.

[3] UNHCR, *Refugee Children. Guidelines on Protection and Care* (Geneva 1994), p. 38.

[4] For more literature see: <http://www.biomedcentral.com/1472-698X/5/7>.

[5] D. SERVAN SCHREIBER, B. LE LIN and B. BIRMAHER, 'Prevalence of Posttraumatic Stress Disorder and Major Depressive Disorder in Tibetan Refugee Children', *Journal of the American Academy of Child & Adolescent Psychiatry* 37:8 (August 1998), pp. 874-879.

Art therapy for children who have experienced war situations or any kind of atrocities is an effective manner through which children can express their fear and anger about what happened to them.[6]

In 1999 the Friends of Tibetan Women's Association *(FOTWA)* started a project called Art Refuge in the Tibetan refugee centres (*TRRC*) in Kathmandu and Dharamsala. The teachers use art as a way of healing the tensions caused by the repressive conditions children had lived under in Tibet, or the high levels of fear and stress suffered on their journey. Art is a way of drawing them out. This project started five years after the first Painting Club at *THF* in Mussoorie, India. The newly arrived children can paint, play and explore their creativity. They can join classes where staff and volunteers offer paints, toys, costumes, time to play, and a place where they get attention and distraction.[7] The book *The Art in Exile* gives a collection of interviews, photographs, and paintings by children in exile.[8] 'It reveals the deep struggle and triumphs of each of these brave and vibrant individuals.'[9]

Tsering Yangchen, one of the teachers at the *TRRC* of Kathmandu, sends four or five stories to FOTWA each month. A postcard with the story and the drawing is sold for the benefit of the refugees.

Drawing in the classroom of TRRC in Kathmandu

In the fall of 1999 Mrs Barbara Hurd spent 5 weeks teaching poetry to children of class VIII to XII at THF. Poetry is seen as the universal language of the heart. All the poems are collected in *Echoes Across the Himalayas. Tibetan Children in Exile* which has never been published as a book, but parts of which have been exhibited in various museums, and a sort of catalogue for this has been made by the photographer Barbara Goodbody. Some of these poems can be read online at <http://www.fotwa.org/artproject/c_exchange/poetry/pagea.html>.

Another similar project took place in 2000 and was called 'Poetry through photography'. Here 21 students from classes VII to IX participated in a 10-week project. It was part of the Cross-Cultural Exchange Program with schools in California and New Mexico sponsored by FOTWA.[10]

---

[6] The Medical Foundation for Victims of Torture, based in the UK, published a booklet for teachers and other educational workers: *Art Therapy in Schools. Working with children who have experienced political violence and torture* (London, 2004). See <http://www.torturecare.org.uk>.
[7] See <http://www.artrefuge.org>.
[8] Sarah K. LUKAS & Friends of Tibetan Women's Association, *The Art in Exile: Paintings by Tibetan Children in India* (Santa Fe, 1998).
[9] See <http://www.fotwa.org>.
[10] See <http://www.fotwa.org/artproject/c_exchange/photography/pagea.html>.

Jetsun Pema, for her part, sees it all in a Buddhist way.

'We believe in karma and we prefer not to look back at suffering. A wound has to heal without interference. I doubt that it is useful to listen to the children and interview them on their sufferings. Is it not better to let them forget progressively?' This was her answer when Western psychologists wanted to interview children whose feet had been amputated, or those who had seen atrocities in their homeland. They wondered how it had affected the children and whether the children showed any suicidal behaviour.[11]

When I was in Dharamsala myself, I asked permission to interview children who joined the school a year ago. A lady in *TCV* Head Office replied:

'We don't want them to be disturbed and moreover for those who still have their parents in Tibet, it can be dangerous.' When I left the office, I remembered Jetsun Pema's words and seeing the children play happily in the courtyard, I thought it was indeed maybe better to leave them be.

Dervla Murphy, an Irish volunteer who worked with Tibetan refugees during the early sixties, writes:

'Observing the happiness of these youngsters I was astonished. I wondered to what extent suspense, loneliness and the memory of past horrors still affected them emotionally. Later, at Dharamsala, I noticed that some of the adolescents and a few adults too, were prone to sudden hysterical outbursts for trivial reasons. Yet on balance it appeared to me that the Tibetans' racial temperament and religious faith did enable them to overcome cheerfully the distresses of a refugee life.'[12]

Most of the time the children indeed adapt easily to their new life, as I could see myself during my visits to several schools in India.

In *TCV* Suja/Bir I met a 10 year-old girl and her younger brother. They had come with their parents to the *Kalachakra*, and once in India their parents had decided to leave the children behind. When the girl heard the news, she said she would throw herself into the river. When I saw both of them two days after their arrival in one of the homes, they already seemed to have adjusted quite well, although nobody can tell what is going on inside their mind.

For some of the children, however, it does not work out.

'Some of them go back after a few months because they cannot adjust: the food is different, they miss their parents, there are some psychological reasons, and the climate is different. They had dreams of going to school, but here there are a lot of rules and they cannot smoke. In Lhasa there is alcohol, drugs, prostitution. Children from the city adapt less easily, they are more spoiled, while those from rural areas appreciate their new life more. Exceptionally, a child runs away. Others have to go back, they

[11] Sophia STRIL-REVER, *Enfants du Tibet*, p. 208.
[12] Dervla MURPHY, *Tibetan Foothold*, p. 21.

have been tortured in Tibet and get ill here. Since in Tibet the climate is cold, diseases don't come out, but here with the hot climate they do.'[13]

I am not a psychologist and it is not my aim to give a deep analysis, but during my interviews I felt that all the children shared the sadness of having lost their country and being away from their parents. Many of the children mentioned that they missed their parents, and especially their mother.

'Children do not develop in isolation: the family is essential in providing the sense of self-esteem, security and identity that is necessary for the child to successfully learn from, and fit into, the rest of the society. (...) The threat to psychosocial well-being is inevitably increased when lengthy or permanent disruptions occur between child and primary care-giver, or child and family. The loss of a mother, particularly at an early age, places a child at a higher psychological risk.'[14]

While conducting most of the interviews in the garden of the clinic of the *TRRC* in Kathmandu, the patients came to know me very well. After a while, some of the children even called me 'ama', mother, 'you are like our mother, because we don't have a mother anymore', one of them told me. Another eight year-old girl, whom I met several times during *Kalachakra*, clung to me every time she saw me and would not let me go. This surprised me, since before I had not spent a lot of time with her. Later I heard her mother was returning to Tibet after 'delivering' her daughter to the *TCV* school. She had felt the farewell with her mother was near, and instinctively she had been seeking affection from another 'ama'. I experienced the same affection in Dharamsala when I met a group of children from the *TRRC* in Kathmandu. One of them jumped on my legs and hugged me affectionately.

It is difficult to stay insensitive.

[13] Interview with Lobsang Choedon, Sponsor Secretary TCV Suja/Bir, December 2005.
[14] UNHCR, *Refugee Children. Guidelines on Protection and Care* (Geneva, 1994), pp. 38-42.

CONCLUSION

It has been my aim to highlight the problem of Tibet's child exodus, to show that it is far from an 'anecdotal' subject. For the last 27 years, counting from when parents began sending their children to India in large numbers, Tibetan children have been denied one of their basic rights: education in their own language; for the last 27 years thousands of children have escaped from Tibet by travelling, mostly by night and often on foot, for days, weeks or months along dangerous, snowbound routes; for the last 27 years some of them have suffered frostbite, fallen ill, or suffered injuries, some have been caught by the police and put in prison, and some even tortured; for the last 27 years an unknown number of them has died on their way to school. And for the last 27 years the world has looked the other way.
I became aware of this problem and did what I felt was my duty: I wrote this book.

Now, in your turn, YOU also know ...

APPENDIX 1: EDUCATION POLICY IN EXILE

'Education is like a weapon;
if properly used
it benefits the individual
and the whole community.'
(H.H. the Dalai Lama)

This is the text of the Basis Education Policy for Tibetans in Exile (BEP), translated from Tibetan. It was formally announced by the *Kashag* on 14 May 2005. It was implemented in a new Tibetan model school in Dharamsala from October 2005 onwards.

CHAPTER I: INTRODUCTION

1. Article 17 (2) of the Charter of Tibetans in Exile, under Directive Principles states: *"Towards enhancing the imparting of education, an ideal education policy meeting the real basic needs of Tibet shall be formulated."* As no such policy has yet been formulated, it is felt that the time is ripe to review the current situation of education of Tibetans in exile and to resolve upon a basic education policy that is better suited to the current needs of the Tibetans in exile and that may serve as a basis for the education policy of Tibet in future when a self-governing status is attained for the whole of the three Cholkhas[1] of Tibet.

CHAPTER II: THE MEANING OF EDUCATION

2.1 Education is to be recognised as a human quality that enables understanding of external objects and phenomena, and that leads to the awakening, maturing and completion of the potential of the inner consciousness.

2.2 Education is not to be recognised as merely grasping what is heard from others. Instead, it is to be recognised as realisation of what is heard through the power of self-confirmation and actualisation of what is realised through persistent contemplation. It is, thus, a process of learning through hearing from others, self-investigation and persistent contemplation.

2.3 Education is to be recognised as a unique inner quality in which the discriminative wisdom and mind-pacifying techniques are conjoined into close partnership.

2.4 Education is to be recognised as a key inner technology that transforms social and personal actions into wholesome deeds.

[1] The three historical regions of Tibet: U-Tsang, Dotod (Kham) and Domed (Amdo); popularly referred to as: U-Tsang, the Cholkha of Dharma; Dotod, the Cholkha of Man; and Domed, the Cholkha of Horse.

2.5 Education is not to be recognised merely as a means of livelihood. Instead it is to be recognised as a means of achieving temporary as well as long-term welfare for the self and others. In particular, it is to be recognised as a vehicle of social welfare and service.

2.6 Education is about recognising the undesired suffering and abandoning its cause; and recognising the desired happiness and engaging in practice of its cause. It is, thus, to be recognised as a means towards engaging in desirable actions and avoiding undesirable actions.

CHAPTER III: THE PURPOSE OF EDUCATION

A. The Purpose of Education in General

3.1 The general purpose of education is to awaken and develop the human qualities of wisdom, loving kindness and compassion; their dependent virtues of right view and conduct; and the art of creativity and innovation.

3.2 To refine human perceptions and sensitivities and to initiate independent and valid investigation into phenomenal and ethical spheres, thus enabling the accomplishment of personal, national and universal goals;

3.3 To empower people and nation to become self-reliant, i.e. without the need to depend on the assistance and support of others; and to generate patriotic and dedicated persons and other resources for achieving the cherished goals of the society and nation.

B. Education for Tibetan People in Particular

3.4 A responsibility the Tibetan people have towards the world community is to preserve and promote the unique wealth of Tibetan culture and traditions, which are of great value to the whole of humanity, through all times and circumstances. Another responsibility the Tibetan people have to the world is to promote and widely propagate the noble principle of Universal Responsibility as introduced and initiated by His Holiness the XIV *Dalai Lama*. These responsibilities are to be fulfilled.

3.5 The ultimate goal of the Tibetan people is to transform the whole of the three Cholkhas of Tibet into a zone of non-violence (ahimsa) and peace; to transform Tibetan society into a non-violent society; and to lead other peoples onto the path of non-violence and compassion. Thus, the Tibetan people must be made capable of correctly and fully understanding the direction, path and means to this goal.

3.6 Tibet is situated on the roof of the world and her wealth of natural resources has a close bearing on the well-being of all Asian nations and the world at large. Thus, it is of paramount importance that the Tibetan people should be able to preserve the natural environment of Tibet.

3.7 A political goal of the Tibetan people is to instill in all Tibetan races of the three Cholkhas the principles of unity, freedom, democracy, rule of law, non-violence, truth and justice. It must be ensured that all Tibetans irrespective of their age properly understand and live by these principles.

3.8 The Tibetan system of economy must also be in accordance with the aforesaid fundamental principles. The Tibetan people must therefore avoid: the two widespread extremes of capitalism and socialism; the two livelihood extremes of luxuriance and destitution; and reliance on wrong means of livelihood[2]. A system ensuring self-sufficiency and right means of livelihood must therefore be followed.

CHAPTER IV: SOURCES OF LEARNING

A. Traditional[3] Tibetan Education

4.1 The principal sources of the traditional Tibetan education are the traditions of Yungdrung Bon[4] and Buddhadharma[5] . Hence, base, path and result, and view, practice and discipline of the inner science contained in these traditions form the core of Tibetan traditional education.

4.2 The four other Tibetan sciences of Language, Valid Cognition,[6] Art and Medicine together with their branches, which have been highly influenced by Bon and Dharma, are also subjects of traditional Tibetan learning.

4.3 The Tibetan Language, which is the medium of these traditional studies, despite its long period of development has undergone very few changes. It holds great potency to communicate intended meaning. It is a great store-house of many profound sciences and arts difficult to be found in other languages. It is, in fact, the only standard base of all Tibetan studies.

B. Modern Education

4.4 Modern Education, unlike traditional Tibetan education, does not trace its origin to a religious or ancient cultural source. It, instead, is a system that was begun and developed in recent centuries by human beings through investigation and experimentation, primarily, on external objects and phenomena. It developed further and was spread more widely in the course of time.

---

[2] Earning a living through means not in accordance with ethical and spiritual principles.

[3] "Tradition" must not be understood as any custom merely perpetuated for a long time. It instead must be understood as a continuum of wisdom or science: (i) originated from a valid source; (ii) passed down through an unbroken lineage; and (iii) supported by valid reasoning. Additionally, it must be an everlasting source of benefit and happiness independent of changes of time and circumstance.

[4] *The earliest native religion of Tibet founded by Shenrab Miwo of Shangshung, the western region of ancient Tibet; more popularly called simply 'Bon'.*

[5] The doctrine and teaching of the Buddha Shakyamuni (623 B.C.-544 B.C.).

[6] *Traditional science of logical reasoning originated from India.*

4.5 Modern Education primarily includes the study of science and technology, mathematics, social sciences, economics, management and planning, and most arts subjects which fall under the category name of "science".

CHAPTER V: THE AIM OF GIVING EDUCATION

5.1 Students must be enabled to fully awaken their discriminative faculty of mind to be able to distinguish right from wrong. This would empower them: to be confident to make decision with freedom of thought and action; to be self-reliant in livelihood, i.e. to live without depending on or exploiting others thereby ensuring their freedom of livelihood by right means; to be able to protect the freedom of the individual and community by non-violence thereby ensuring the freedom of security. This constitutes the principle of ***"freedom".***

5.2 By embracing other beings as more precious than the self and sacrificing the self for the service and welfare of other persons, the noble spirit of altruism is to be generated and established. This constitutes the principle of ***"altruism".***

5.3 For the sake of future generations, the environment and natural resources must be conserved for the peaceful sustenance of this planet, and people must be empowered to uphold their ancestral cultural heritage. This ability to preserve culture and environment constitutes the principle of ***"upholding the heritage".***

5.4 In relation to the general well-being of the world and in accordance with the needs of time and place, we must be able to introduce new principles, systems, objects, movements and so forth. This constitutes the principle of ***"innovation".*** Raising citizens to be endowed with these four stated qualities shall be the aim of giving education.

CHAPTER VI: SYSTEM OF EDUCATION

6.1 A system of education having traditional Tibetan education as its core and modern education as its essential co-partner shall be implemented.

6.2 As nothing is more important than the teacher in the work of imparting education, a teacher-centred education system shall be followed.

6.3 However, when teachers actually undertake the work of teaching, the student-centred methodology shall be followed.

6.4 In an education system having traditional education as its core, it is appropriate to have the medium in which the traditional learning abides as the medium of instruction for general education. Hence, efforts shall be made to gradually convert the medium of instruction in all Tibetan institutions of learning from the pre-primary level up to the highest research study level, into Tibetan language.

6.5 Inherent to traditional as well as modern learning, is the content meaning and the vehicle that conveys it. As proficiency in the vehicle of speech is gained with the study of language and proficiency in content meaning is gained with the study of Valid Cognition (pramana), the Tibetan language and Valid Cognition shall be taught with special emphasis at the basic school level.

6.6 In order to empower students to investigate and reflect on obscure phenomena and to develop confidence in presenting their findings after investigation before the world's scholars, the process of learning by hearing and thinking as indicated by Tibetan Inner Science shall be widely introduced and promoted.

6.7 In order to instill into pupils the principles of wholesome thought and conduct from the pre-primary school level, the quality and role of teachers, formation of school curriculum, and methodology of teaching shall be framed mainly in accordance with the traditional Tibetan principles and sciences, rather than the modern system.

6.8 A standard system of education, in which school and university graduates can freely follow their family occupations or start a new occupation of their choice, shall be introduced. This will help prevent the situation of producing large flocks of unemployed graduates.

CHAPTER VII: THE STRUCTURE OF BASIC EDUCATION

7.1 Education is a life-long process to be pursued and practised by persons of all ages. Of the two systems of education, formal and non-formal, primary importance shall be given to the latter.

7.2 Nevertheless, since formal education has become important and necessary in the present day, the Administration shall frame a general structure covering all citizens as part of the education policy and issue directives accordingly.

7.3 The monastic centres and other institutions of traditional learning shall not come under the purview of the structure framed by the Administration. However, if such institutions and other societies or individuals establish schools for general basic education and desire recognition from the Tibetan Administration in exile, they must conform to the general structure.

7.4 The structure of the basic education shall comprise of a four-level school system: (1) three-year pre-primary school; (2) five-year primary school up to the fifth class; (3) three-year middle school up to the eighth class; and (4) four-year secondary school up to the twelfth class. Until a new system suitable for Tibetans is introduced for the three-year pre-primary level, the Montessori system shall be followed.

7.5 The pursuit of further secondary school education or vocational studies after graduating from Class X shall be decided by individual choice and prescribed academic requirements. Likewise, after graduating from Class XII, opportunities for the pursuit of vocational studies by choice shall be made available.

CHAPTER VIII: SUBJECTS OF STUDY

A. Tibetan Language

8.1 The studies of language and grammar being the basis of, and gateway to, any learning, the Tibetan language, grammar and literature shall be the main subject of study from the pre-primary level to Class XII.

B. Science of Valid Cognition

8.2 The ability to penetrate deeply into subjects and into the nature of phenomena through independent investigation and search, without blindly following the word of others, can be developed from the study of Science of Valid Cognition. The teaching of this subject up to Class XII with special stress shall therefore be recognised as one of the most important directives.

C. Other Languages & Valid Cognition Sciences

8.3 A three-language policy shall be adopted. Besides the primary mother-tongue language, a student should be fully proficient in any one foreign language and acquire a working knowledge of reading and writing in a third language after graduating from Class X. A second language may be chosen from among the four languages of Hindi, Chinese, English and Spanish. Depending on the availability of facilities more choices may be given. However, until such time when the medium of instruction is fully converted to the mother tongue, English will remain by necessity the second language. Hence the above stated choice of the second language cannot be implemented immediately, but such a long-term aim should be established now. The third language will be the language of the region where the school is located. If the regional language is Tibetan or the second language, any other essential language may be chosen in their place.

8.4 From the pre-primary level and up to Class III, no other language besides Tibetan shall be taught. Even the teaching of terms in, and songs of, other language should be avoided. The teaching of second and third languages shall be started from Class IV and Class VI respectively.

8.5 Suitable introductory studies of: the modern sciences of logical reasoning; experimental methodology; tenets or theories of the social sciences; and the investigative methodologies used in the study of history shall be included within the curriculum of the middle school (Class VI - VIII).

D. Art & Crafts

8.6 The study of any sustainable art or craft of a non-violent and environmentally friendly nature shall be made compulsory at both the levels of middle school (Class VI to VIII) and secondary school (Class IX to XII). For this purpose, a variety of traditional art and crafts of Tibetan and Indian origin and, to a lesser extent, certain modern art and crafts - suitable to our situation and qualifying the above characteristics - shall be taught in the schools. Depending on the availability of facilities and the interest of students, the study of a suitable art or craft may be included within the curriculum of the primary school level also. Similarly, for development of special talents and skills in art and crafts, language and other studies, suitable subjects of study may also be included in the curriculum according to the interest and mental disposition of the students.

8.7 Several vocational schools shall be established for the admission of students who have graduated from Class X and Class XII. Besides the main training courses of Tibetan art and crafts, and various modern art and crafts, the Tibetan language and another additional language shall also be taught in these schools up to an appropriate level.

E. Science & Humanities

8.8 The introduction of general science; social sciences; history; sciences of mind; and other subjects of science and arts that are necessary shall be included in the study curriculum of the middle school (Class VI to VIII) for a length of time, and up to a level suitable for this stage.

F. Mathematics

8.9 Since study of mathematics is both useful in general life and essential for the study of science, adequate study of modern mathematics and an elementary introduction to traditional Tibetan mathematics shall be included in the school curriculum.

G. Principles of Non-Violence and Democracy

8.10 The study of the value, teachings, practices and histories of the principles of non-violence and democracy shall be suitably included within the study curricula of all three levels of school - primary, middle and secondary - in accordance with the degree of understanding of students at those levels.

H. Moral Conduct

8.11 Morality is not to be taught as a separate subject. Instead it is of vital importance to closely connect it to the central theme of all educational activities and especially all subjects of study to be taught in the classroom. However, excerpts from religious sources on morality; stories and tales on spiritual themes; traditional writings on social or secular ethics; and biographies of ancient and contemporary great personalities should be included within the content of school textbooks or supplementary reading.

I. Physical Exercise & Sports

8.12 Since school students are undergoing both physical and mental growth, it is important to dedicate equal attention and time to their health, hygiene and physical training and to their academic curriculum. Training in various forms of Tibetan traditional physical exercise; physical training of yoga; breathing exercises of pranayama and so forth should be given. Additionally, natural health treatments such as baths, massage, lotion application and so forth should be introduced from the primary school level. Similarly, manual work and walking being principal modes of physical exercise, a definite period of time should be allotted for them within the regular timetable. For diversion and recreation of students, games and sports shall also be included in the curriculum. Whilst attaching more importance to the traditional Tibetan games and sports, training in contemporary games and sports shall also be given.

J. Subjects of Study for Secondary School

8.13 In the common four-year study curriculum, it is necessary for the time being to retain all subjects of study prescribed for Class X and Class XII Examinations of the host country. Even after division of classes into science and other streams, Tibetan language and Science of Valid Cognition must continue to be included in the curriculum as compulsory subjects for all streams and classes of this level.

CHAPTER IX: SYLLABI & DURATION

9.1 Curricula and syllabi for all classes up to Class XII shall be prepared in the order and inter-related manner as required by the Basic Education Policy. For that purpose a special committee shall be established to prepare the Common School Curricula and Syllabi.

CHAPTER X: EXAMINATIONS

10.1 The present system of evaluation by means of a two or three hour examination shall be discarded. Promotion of students to the next class, up to Class VIII, shall be done,not on the basis of the present system of examination, but rather on the basis of the collective decision of concerned teachers through an overall assessment of student's regular conduct, level of understanding, practical skill and classroom participation. However, for the time being and until further review, the system of written examinations may continue with a 50 percent share of the overall evaluation. A new system of evaluation shall also be introduced to estimate the standard of learning for the classes of the secondary school, with the exception of those who are required to sit Board Examinations of the host country.

CHAPTER XI: TEACHERS

11.1 The future of any society rests on the quality of education provided, and the quality of education in turn depends on the quality of the teachers. Thus, teachers being the most important persons in society, great effort shall be made to recruit persons of highest character and learning to the profession. Legal provisions shall be put in place to ensure that due recognition and commensurate benefits are given to teachers.

11.2 Within the public service cadres, a separate cadre for persons in educational service shall be created. Rank and honour of this service division shall be superior to those of all other public service divisions.

11.3 Teachers should possess the general qualities of knowledge and experience as indicated by the contemporary educational system and inner qualities such as motivation and moral attitude as indicated by the traditional Tibetan sources. New schemes shall be devised and established to cultivate as many qualified teachers as possible on a regular basis.

11.4 Teachers must follow a life-long learning career and remain fully committed to the teaching profession. Resources towards the fulfillment of these conditions shall be provided.

11.5 All teachers employed at pre-primary to secondary school levels must have successfully undergone teacher training courses. The training should not only be on contemporary subjects and teaching methodology but also contain instructions on the qualities and characteristics that behoove a teacher and methods of cultivation of pupils as given in the traditional sources. History of traditional Tibetan education shall also be included in the training course.

11.6 In order to train teachers in contemporary as well as traditional teaching courses, a scheme for training Tibetan teachers shall be implemented.

11.7 Clinical teaching practice for trainees for a definite period of time at any college or other teaching institution shall be recognised as a vital and important part of the training course.

11.8 In order to maintain proper scrutiny over the quality of teachers, it shall be made mandatory for both qualified teacher-candidates and currently employed teachers to receive a five-year teaching license from the Tibetan Council of Education. This license must be renewed every five years. During that period, it shall be required for teachers to complete a certain number of in-service training courses enhancing professional development as a pre-requisite for renewal of the teaching license.

11.9 Comprehensive rules and regulations governing recruitment, salary and benefits, promotion and transfer, regular and additional duties, code of conduct, welfare and accountability shall be framed.

11.10 Teachers being leaders of people and nation building, adequate facilities and an environment conducive to their unobstructed development in freedom of thought, power of intellect and spirit of innovation, must be provided.

11.11 Teachers are to be role models in character for students and should be able to instill wholesome qualities into their students. For this reason, policy shall be framed against the recruitment of persons with low moral character as teachers, even if they possess high academic qualifications.

11.12 Based on the importance and need of pre-primary learning, a Class XII graduate withrequisite training shall be appointed as assistant teacher for each of the pre-primary classes. Priority shall be given to female candidates for the posts of pre-primary teacher and assistant. The pre-primary and primary teachers should possess the minimum qualification of a Bachelor Degree and must have completed a teacher 12 education course. Their salary and benefits shall be same as those of teachers of the secondary school level.

CHAPTER XII: ADMINISTRATION

12.1 All Tibetan schools in exile are required to uniformly implement the policies and directive guidelines on policies as and when framed by the Tibetan Administration in exile with respect to aims and objectives, structure, curriculum, evaluation, teacher and management of education.

12.2 The Department of Education, *CTA* is the highest central administrative authority in the affairs of education of Tibetans in exile. It shall implement the education policies as and when framed by the Central Tibetan Administration either directly, or principally through the medium of autonomous organisations.

12.3 It is emphasised that the internal management of schools shall be done principally by the local organisations and that the schools do not depend or rely on the Central Administration or their own central organisations in that matter.

12.4 To advise the Tibetan administration in exile on education policy; to monitor implementation of the education policy; to grant recognition and approval to rules and regulations, curriculum, textbook composition and examination system of all Tibetan schools in exile after necessary inspection; to grant recognition to all schools including pre-primary schools after necessary inspection; to issue and renew teaching licenses; and to monitor and oversee educational affairs as a whole, a permanent body **'*The Education Council of Tibetans in Exile*'** shall be established.

12.5 For the construction of plans on teacher education system; school curriculum and text books; teaching methodology; and other teaching resources, committees and task forces of scholars and experts shall be established and appointed as necessary from time to time.

12.6 Autonomous and private schools may seek and receive recognition for their schools from the Central Tibetan Administration. The Department of Education shall lay down provisions and frame regulations for granting recognition to such schools.

12.7 All schools recognised by the Central Tibetan Administration shall abide by the provisions of structure and mandatory curriculum as framed by this policy. However, the autonomous and private schools may decide independently as to how the details of the policy are implemented.

CHAPTER XIII: RIGHT TO EDUCATION

A. Basic Education

13.1 All Tibetan citizens performing citizen's duties shall have the right to basic education up to Class XII free of tuition fee and without any discrimination on the basis of sex, race, religion, place of origin, being rich or poor, being ordained or lay.

13.2 No Tibetan parent shall have the power to prevent a child between the ages of 6 and 16 years of age from attending school. In order to maintain good relationship between parents and children, special emphasis shall be laid on children staying with their parents and on not admitting young children to boarding schools.

13.3 In order to facilitate the completion of studies up to Class X by all children, opportunity for re-admission to school shall be given to the students who were obliged to leave their schools before finishing Class X.

13.4 Only those Class X graduates with promising academic records - to be determined by a thorough assessment of teacher's evaluation report, examination results and interest and intelligence of individual students – shall be admitted to the secondary school education.

13.5 The remaining Class X graduates may be allowed to pursue vocational training courses for two years according to their wish. All Class X graduates shall have right to follow these training courses.

B. Education through Self-Learning

13.6 Students who have failed admission to the secondary school after Class X can however continue the secondary school studies through self-learning during or after their vocational training. Necessary provisions for such modes of learning shall be made.

C. Students with Special Needs

13.7 Best efforts shall be made to educate students with special needs in regular schools together with other students. All schools must therefore make provision for all necessary facilities to meet the needs of such students. Teachers must also be provided with standard in-service training both physically and mentally for education of students with special needs.

13.8 One or two special schools with complete facilities shall be separately established for the students who cannot be admitted in regular schools due to serious physical and/or mental disabilities. These schools shall be equipped with teachers and staffs who are fully trained in special education. Provisions shall be made for students in these separately established schools to maintain close contact with their family and community.

CHAPTER XIV: INTERIM PROVISION

14.1 It is difficult to immediately accomplish the provision of all teaching and non-teaching personnel as required by the new policy. For this reason, there is no doubt that the complete implementation of the above stated policies will take a considerable period of time. Therefore, to the end of achieving the ultimate aims of these policies in a gradual manner, a definite action plan shall be drawn after adoption of this policy in order to effect organised and gradual changes in the existing system and to implement the new policy.

14.2 To serve as model and for gathering experience, one or two new schools shall be opened as soon as possible wherein the provisions of the new education policy shall be fully implemented.

14.3 A committee shall be established for the functions of: selection of teacher candidates; conception of training schemes for such candidates; prescription of curricula and text books; and the drawing up of other academic plans. The above work plans (mentioned in this chapter) shall be started within the calendar year of 2005.

CHAPTER XV: REVIEW

15.1 A committee of scholars and experts, to be appointed by the Department of Education, shall periodically review and revaluate the plan of action for implementing the policy.

15.2 Articles of this policy may be reviewed whenever necessary.

Source: <http://www.tcewf.org>. Educational policy. Basis Education Policy for Tibetans in Exile (BEP).

APPENDIX 2: TWO MORE STORIES

'There is no freedom of body, speech and mind.'
(Anonymous refugee)

In Amaravati (India) during *Kalachakra* (January 2006) I met two men who eagerly wanted to tell me their story. Even if neither of them was still a child, I decided to publish their account because it contains information about the difficulties they and others faced in Tibet, and because I wanted to give them a wider voice. Their names, places of birth, and the name of the second interviewee's prison have been concealed in order to protect their identity.

'I am 29 years old and I am from Kham region. My family is a poor family of nomads, so I never went to school. I studied Tibetan language on my own while I was looking after the animals. At 16 I became a monk and I went to the monastery. In the beginning of 2003 I wrote some books; one was about the future of Tibet, so I gave my point of view about our lost freedom and politics. On 2 June of that same year the police came and took all my books and PC. Luckily I had still one copy since I had given one to a friend. They brought me to prison and interrogated me; then they charged me two years: one for writing about the reduction of freedom and one year for writing about politics. They also beat me. In prison you know they eat meat and I had been a vegetarian for a long time. One day in June 2005 I became very angry because I had already asked them several times to give me something else to eat. They took me and brought me to a cell where I was beaten with an electric stick on my legs, face and whole body. On 22 July I was released from prison and I decided to escape. I started my journey on 12 December, by bus to Lhasa. There I stayed for two, three days. Then with six people we started by foot, and on the way we met three more people from Amdo. We walked for ten days; three days we had to cross the snow: sometimes the snow came up to our knees, sometimes up to our armpits. Luckily we had warm clothes and we wore plastic bags around our legs to avoid frostbite. We could find our way very easily thanks to a map given us by someone in the monastery. When we arrived at the border, there were police on both sides of the road: Bhutanese[1] and Chinese police. So we travelled by night and I remember we were all very scared. We heard all kind of stories about Tibetans who had to face big difficulties on their way, like frostbitten fingers and toes. One girl from Golok (Amdo), she died, she was frozen to death. This all gave me the strength to continue. We reached India and afterwards we went further by jeep. First five of us, then the jeep returned to take the four others. It took us two days to reach Delhi. From there we went to Dharamsala, then down here to *Kalachakra*. I don't know yet what I am going to do: stay here or return home; first I want to see His Holiness before taking my decision.'

'I am from Golok in Amdo. I was an only child. My family and all Tibetans were suffering so much, but you simply could not tell it to somebody. It was too dangerous;

[1] The border he mentions is the border between Tibet and Bhutan. The mountain they climbed was in the area of Lhodrak, near Bhutan.

you could not even trust your neighbours. When the Chinese came, they destroyed or took all the belongings of rich families. My mother had to undergo thamzing;[2] they asked her a lot of questions every week. My father died because the Chinese had taken everything, even our food.

Tibetans like luxury dresses. Sometimes the Chinese borrow these clothes and afterwards they say that these are 'made in China'. They want to pretend that Tibetans are very happy. 'We made them rich,' they say, but behind there is so much suffering that is never shown to the tourists. Tibetans are really very poor.

A lot of Tibetans are nomads. The Chinese force them to go to the city and say they will help to buy a house. A house might cost 5,000 *Yuan*, but they make them pay more and then put this money in their pocket. In fact, these nomads cannot afford this, so they have to loan money from the bank. Afterwards they are not able to pay their loan back and then they go to jail. Some of the nomads have lots of animals: *yaks* and goats. The Chinese encourage them to sell their cattle, because the money they receive, they can put in the bank and they can also buy food with it. But before they lived from the animals; if they put their money on the bank, in one month it can be finished. The Chinese sometimes advise nomads to come and live in a house in China, afterwards they start digging for natural resources on their land. They also force drokpas (nomads) to put up a fence; first they say it's for free, but afterwards they charge 20,000 or 50,000 *Yuan*. Chinese charge everything: the land, *yaks*, butter.

When parents don't send their children to school, they are fined perhaps 5,000 *Yuan*. Thus children go to school but they only learn Chinese and bad things, like taking alcohol or smoking. Parents are very disappointed about this. Children are often beaten at school, sometimes they even die and parents cannot complain to anybody. Sometimes rich families pay the school fees for poor families, but they don't send their own children because the quality of the schools is so bad.

When Tibetans have no children, this is very good. When parents have two or three children, they are fined. They want to destroy the Tibetan generation. If no more babies, then afterwards there will be no more Tibetans. Chinese also want Tibetans to mix with them, then slowly, slowly our culture, language, everything will disappear.

I have wanted to come to see His Holiness for more than 20 years. I fled in 2001 together with three families; we were a group of 20 people. We came from Amdo to Lhasa. My son knew a guide since he came already a few times before. Each of us paid the guide 1,600 *Yuan* to get us to the border; we did it by jeep and during the night. To cross the border, it took us two nights by foot and we had to pay another guide 3,000 *Rupees*. From there to Kathmandu we hid in a truck full of clothes, so it was difficult to breathe. Again we had to pay 3,000 *Rupees* to somebody to get into this truck.

When I arrived in India I met one of my neighbours. In Tibet we had never spoken to each other about our life. In Tibet there is no freedom of religion, of thinking about His Holiness; no freedom of body, speech and mind. It is such a big difference with here.'

---

[2] Thamzing: struggle-session; a method of interrogation combined with force often used by the Chinese. It is used in prisons as well as to 're-educate' ordinary people.

GLOSSARY

This list contains all the words written in *italics* in the text that needed an explanation.

Amala: ama is the Tibetan word for mother. Amala is a respectful form, which is used for a mother as well as for an older woman. Jetsun Pema, the younger sister of the Dalai Lama and president of the TCV is called Amala.

Bodh Gaya: an important historical city since it is seen as the place of the enlightenment of the first Buddha Shakyamuni. It is also the site of annual week-long Buddhist teachings given by the Dalai Lama.

CRC = Convention on the Rights of the Child. This UN Convention was adopted on 20 November 1989 and entered into force on 2 September 1990. It has been ratified by all countries except the USA and Somalia. The full text of the CRC can be found on the website of Office of the United Nations High Commissioner for Human Rights (OHCHR): <http://www.ohchr.org/>.

CTA = Central Tibetan Administration was first established on 29 April 1959 in Mussoorie (India) as the continuation of the government of independent Tibet. In May 1960 the CTA was moved to Dharamsala and it is now located in an area named Gangchen Kyishong, which means "Happy valley of snow". It is recognized by Tibetans, both within and outside Tibet, as their sole and legitimate government. The CTA functions according to the modern democratic principles of its constitution, which was adopted by the Assembly of Tibetan People's Deputies.[1] <http://www.tibet.net>.

Dalai Lama: the highest temporal and spiritual authority in Tibet. He belongs to the Buddhist Gelukpa tradition, the so-called Yellow Hat sect. Dalai Lama is a Mongolian title which means 'Ocean of Wisdom'. He is seen as the manifestation of Chenrezig, the Boddhisattva of Compassion. Boddhisattvas are enlightened beings who have postponed their own nirvana and chosen to take rebirth to serve humanity.[2] When he dies, he reincarnates as a young child. At this moment the XIVth Dalai Lama, Tenzin Gyatso, is 70 years old and has lived in exile in India since 1959. In 1989 he received the Nobel Peace Prize. In accordance with Tibetan custom the Dalai Lama, the Panchen Lama and the Karmapa are addressed as His Holiness (H.H.).

Dal bhat: a typical Nepalese dish which is made up of lentil soup, rice, and curried vegetables. Most Nepalese eat it twice a day.

DIIR= Department of Information and International Relations of the Tibetan government in exile in Dharamsala. <http://www.tibet.net/>

[1] Information sheet of the Department of Information and International Relations of the Tibetan government in exile in Dharamsala. (DIIR)

[2] See <http://www.tibet.net/>: Biography of H.H. the Dalai Lama.

DOI = Department of Immigration; one of the partners of the 'gentlemen's agreement'.

ICT = International Campaign for Tibet is a non-profit membership organization that monitors and promotes internationally recognized human rights in Tibet. ICT was founded in 1988 and has offices in Washington D.C., Berlin and Amsterdam. <http://www.savetibet.org>.

Kalachakra: an initiation, teaching given by the *Dalai Lama*. In 2006 it was given in Amaravati in the state of Andrah Pradesh (South India), where 2,500 years ago Buddha gave his first teaching. Kalachakra is the Sanskrit word for 'Wheel of time', which can also be translated as 'Cycle of Time'.

Karmapa: the leader of the Kagyupa school in Tibetan Buddhism. The 17th Karmapa, Urgyen Trinley, had been recognized by China and was showcased as an example of the Chinese policy of tolerance towards religious persons. In January 2000 he escaped to India, making a laughing stock of China. In the beginning China stuck to the version that he had left to seek some ritual objects in India and would return when he had obtained them. In 2001 India granted him the status of refugee.

Kashag: is the highest executive body of the Tibetan exile community. It can be compared with a cabinet. The head of the Kashag is known as Kalon Tripa.

LWF = *Lutheran World Federation* was founded in Sweden in 1947 and has its headquarters in Geneva. LWF is an international church organization active in humanitarian work. The Department for World Service (DWS), the international relief, rehabilitation and development agency of LWF, provides services in, among others, the fields of education, health, vocational skills for income generation, and community infrastructure. Its work includes issues such as the environment, human rights, land mines, refugees, training, evaluation, development education, and migration and resettlement.
LWF, already active and working with a range of international partners in Nepal, has since 31 October replaced TRWO as UNHCR's partner in the management of the TRRC. <http://www.lutheranworld.org>

Ngawang Sangdrol: was arrested at the age of 13 together with other nuns after a peaceful demonstration in Lhasa in 1990. She was imprisoned for nine months without charge. On 17 June 1992 she was rearrested for staging a peaceful demonstration along with other nuns and monks. Despite her adolescence, she was sentenced to three years and incarcerated in the Drapchi prison, the most infamous and severe prison in Lhasa. After recording an audio tape with patriotic songs and smuggling it out of the prison together with a brief biography, she and the so-called 'Drapchi 14 singing nuns' were badly tortured and their sentences extended by six years. Ngawang Sangdrol was finally released in 2002 thanks to an international campaign and is working for ICT in Washington. For more details: <http://www.savetibet.org/campaigns/politicalprisoners/ngawangsangdrol>.

NGO = Non-Governmental Organization, an organization that is not part of the local or state or federal government; often involved in humanitarian aid.

Panchen Lama: is an influential spiritual teacher of the Gelukpa tradition in Tibetan Buddhism. He is often wrongly called the second highest spiritual authority in Tibet.[3] In May 1995 the *Dalai Lama* announced that Gedhun Choekyi Nyima, a six year-old child, had been recognized as the reincarnation of the Xth Panchen Lama. Shortly after this, China abducted the child and chose an alternative, Gyaltsen Norbu, as the 11th Panchen Lama. Until now, despite international pressure, the fate of the child and his abducted parents is uncertain.

Rupees: Nepal's currency (=NRs). €1 is about 84 NRs.

Sherpas: a people living in the mountains of eastern and central Nepal, most of their villages are above 2500m, but they are originally from Tibet. They settled in the area about 500 years ago. Sherpas came to international prominence when in 1953 the Mt. Everest team (Sir Edmund Hillary) hired them. **S**herpas are members of an ethnic group, while **s**herpa is a trekking guide or a mountaineer. Many sherpas are Sherpas, and they have won worldwide fame for their skill, hardiness and loyalty.[4]

Stupa: a Buddhist religious monument that represents the origin and centre of the world. It is a solid reliquary mound derived from the ancient tumuli of India. The levels of the stupa symbolize the macrocosm of the five elements (the base is earth, the dome water, the spire fire, the parasol capital air, the finial ether or Buddha nature), and the microcosm of the human nervous system, the five principal chakras and the five senses.[5]

Thanka: a Tibetan Buddhist painting used as wall decoration. Its origin goes back to the 7th or 8th century during the reign of King Songtsen Gampo. Painted on cotton or silk brocade, it contains sacred colours and it can be rolled up. Its form is always rectangular and the subjects can be Buddha, a mandala, gods and goddesses, the wheel of life. It is a visual support for meditation in monasteries or at home.

TAR = Tibet Autonomous Region. Tibet traditionally comprised three main areas: Amdo (north-eastern Tibet), Kham (eastern Tibet) and U-Tsang (central and western Tibet). The TAR was set up by the Chinese government in 1965 and covers the areas of Tibet west of the Yangzi river, including a part of Kham. The rest of Kham and Amdo have been incorporated into Chinese provinces, and designated autonomous counties. Most of Qinghai and parts of Sichuan and Yunnan provinces are acknowledged by the Chinese as 'Tibetan'.[6]

---

[3] Dhundup GYALPO, 'Plagiarising Propaganda', in *Tibetan Bulletin. The Official Journal of the Tibetan Administration*, Vol. 9, Issue 2 (March-April 2005), p. 34. Under the Dalai Lama are the heads of the four schools of Tibetan Buddhism and Bon, all of whom enjoy equal rank and authority.

[4] *Lonely Planet Guide Nepal*, 2003, p. 27; Stan ARMINGTON, *Trekking in the Nepal Himalaya* (Victoria, Australia, 2001), pp. 40-41.

[5] Alistair SHEARER, *Buddha. The Intelligent Heart* (London, 1997), pp. 74-75.

[6] Alternative Report for the Committee on the Rights of the Child, p. 43.

TCHRD = Tibetan Centre for Human Rights and Democracy, an independent centre which aims to promote and protect human rights and a democratic policy for Tibet. TCHRD started in 1996 and has its office in Dharamsala. <http://www.tchrd.org>.

TCV = Tibetan Children's Villages, a network of boarding schools under the authority of H.H. Dalai Lama to take care of the Tibetan refugee children. Started in the early sixties and is part of the SOS Children's Villages (see chapter 9). <http://www.tcv.org.in> or <http://www.tcewf.org> (TCEWF = Tibetan Children's Educational Welfare and Fund).

THF = Tibetan Homes Foundation, started in 1962 in Mussoorie to take care of the Tibetan refugee children. Today there are two branches, one in Mussoorie and one in Rajpur (see chapter 9). <http://www.tibhomes.org>.

Tibetan flag: the present national flag was designed by the XIIIth Dalai Lama. The white triangle represents a snow mountain and symbolizes Tibet, known as the land of snow; the six red rays emanating from the sun symbolize the six original tribes of Tibet: the Se, Mu, Dong, Tong, Dru, and Ra; the red and blue rays alternate with each other to symbolize the unflinching determination of Tibet's two protector deities (Nechung and Sri Devi) to guard the country's spiritual and secular traditions; the sun symbolizes the equal enjoyment of freedom, as well as spiritual and secular well-being; the pair of snow lions symbolize the complete victory of the spiritual and secular ruling government; the raised jewel symbolizes Tibet's reverence for the three Precious Gems: the Buddha, the Dharma (teaching), and the Sangha (community of monks and nuns); the three-coloured circular motif held by the lions symbolizes adherence to the Ten Divine Virtues and Sixteen Human Moral Code; the three-sided yellow border represents the flourishing of Buddha's teachings. The side without border represents Tibet's openness to non-Buddhist thought.[7]

Tibet Office: a Tibet Office is an official agency of H.H. Dalai Lama and *CTA*. The one mentioned in the text is situated in Kathmandu. It was set up in 1960 with two objectives: dealing with any issues related to Tibetans in Nepal and maintaining close relations between the Nepalese government and the Tibetan government-in-exile. All Tibetan institutions in Nepal including refugee settlements, handicrafts centres fall under his jurisdiction. The Representative is appointed directly by the Dalai Lama and works as a centralized authority with which officials at the Ministry of Home Affairs can discuss problems that arise concerning Tibetans in Nepal whether related to new arrivals or to those residing permanently in the settlements.[8]
There are Tibet Offices world-wide: in Delhi, New York, Geneva, Tokyo, London, Canberra, Moscow, Pretoria, Taipei and Paris, and in Brussels the EU Co-ordination Office. <http://www.tibet.net/> (the official site of *CTA*)

TIN = Tibet Information Network was an independent news and research service that started in the late eighties providing information and analysis of the current political, economic, social, environmental and human rights situation in Tibet. It stopped its ac-

[7] ICT website & information brochure of CTA, *An Introduction to CTA*, pp. 17-18.
[8] *Tibet's Stateless Nationals*, p. 111.

tivities in September 2005 and unfortunately the archives can no longer be accessed. Tibet Info Net was created immediately afterwards and provides the same sort of information service. <http://www.tininfonet.net>.

TJC = Tibet Justice Center, formerly known as International Committee of Lawyers for Tibet, was established in 1989. <http://www.tibetjustice.org>

TRRC = Tibetan Refugee Reception Centre. In Kathmandu (Nepal) as well as in Delhi and Dharamsala (India) these centres receive the new arrivals from Tibet. In the TRRC of Kathmandu refugees are registered by the UNHCR and they get the necessary travel documents to transit to India (see chapters 7 and 8).

TRWO = The Tibetan Refugee Welfare Office, which opened 40 years ago. It has the social function of looking after the welfare of the Tibetans (their education, health, etc.). It acts as the local partner of UNHCR and provides most of the practical assistance required by newly arrived refugees. It manages the flux of refugees transiting through the TRRC.

Tsampa: is made of roasted barley flour with butter tea poured over it. It is very nutritious and widely eaten by Tibetans.

TWA = Tibetan Women Association was originally founded in Tibet on 12 March 1959, when thousands of women gathered in Lhasa to protest peacefully against the Chinese occupation. Many of them were arrested, imprisoned, tortured and beaten without trial. On 10 September 1984, the TWA was officially reinstated with 12 branches in India. Today TWA has branches world-wide. Its main objective is to raise awareness of the abuses faced by Tibetan women in Tibet. <http://www.tibetanwomen.org>.

UNHCR = the United Nations High Commissioner for Refugees. It was established in December 1950 to help the more than one million European refugees uprooted by World War II. Today it functions as one of the world's principal humanitarian agencies. The headquarters of UNHCR are in Geneva. In 1991 UNHCR opened an office in Nepal; since that time they have been involved in the transit procedure of newly arriving refugees (under the 'gentlemen's agreement'), they monitor missions to the border to 'educate' the local authorities in the proper treatment of newly arriving refugees. UNHCR provides the total funds of the TRRC and assists Tibetans living in Nepal (see chapter 7). <http://www.unhcr.org>.

Yak: an animal living on the Tibetan plateau. It has a long shaggy coat that reaches almost to the ground. Tibetans use its wool (for clothes) and skin (for tents) and eat its meat. Yak butter is used in the Tibetan salted tea.

Yuan: Chinese currency. The only legal tender in Tibet. A Yuan is worth about €10.

A SELECTIVE BIBLIOGRAPHY

BOOKS

Asia Watch, Detained in China and Tibet. A Directory of Political and Religious Prisoners (New York, Washington, Los Angeles, London, 1994).

Catriona BASS, *Education in Tibet. Policy & Practice since 1950* (London, 1998).

Maria BLUMENCRON, *Vlucht over de Himalaya,* (Byblos/Roularta, 2003).

Carlo BULDRINI, *A Long Way from Tibet* (New Delhi, 2005).

Hari BANSH JHA, *Tibetans in Nepal* (Delhi, 1992).

Federica de CESCO, *Witte kraanvogel boven Tibet* (Antwerp, 2001).

From the Roof of the World: Refugees of Tibet (Berkeley, Cal., 1992).

Patrick FRENCH, *Younghusband. Last Great Imperial Adventurer* (London, 1994).

Melvyn C. GOLDSTEIN, with the help of Gelek Rimpoche, *A History of Modern Tibet, 1913-1951. The Demise of the Lamaist State* (Berkeley, Los Angeles, and London, 1989).

Reginald HOYAUX, *25 eeuwen Tibet. Van Boeddha tot Deng Xiaoping* (Antwerp, 1996).

John Kenneth KNAUS, *Orphans of the Cold War* (New York, 1999).

Claude B. LEVENSON, *La Messagère du Tibet. Le Retour du panchen-lama* (Arles, 1997).

Sarah K. LUKAS & Friends of Tibetan Women's Association, *The Art in Exile: Paintings by Tibetan Children in India* (Santa Fe, 1998).

Dervla MURPHY, *Tibetan Foothold* (New Delhi, 1988).

Dawa NORBU, *China's Tibet Policy* (Richmond, 2001).

Olivier PAPEGNIES & Nicolas BOURLAKOFF, *Tibetains: 'De Lhassa à Dharamsala'* (Jumet, 2001).

Jetsun PEMA, *Tibet. My story. An Autobiography* (UK, 1998).

Andrew J. POLLARD & David R. MURDOCK, *The High Altitude Medicine Handbook* (Micro Edition, India, 1997).

J. RUSSELL, *Dharamsala. Tibetan Refuge* (Torrance CA, 2000).

Tsering SHAKYA, *The Dragon in the Land of Snows. A History of Modern Tibet since 1947* (London, 1999).

Jonathan SPENCE, *In Search of Modern China* (2nd edition, New York and London, 1999).

Sophia STRIL-REVER, *Enfants du Tibet. De coeur à coeur avec Jetsun Pema et soeur Emmanuelle* (Paris, 2000).

Tanka B. SUBBA, Flight and Adaptation. *Tibetan Refugees in the Darjeeling-Sikkim Himalaya* (Dharamsala, 1990).

Tibet Justice Center, *Tibet's Stateless Nationals: Tibetan Refugees in Nepal* (Berkeley, Cal., 2002).

ARTICLES IN MAGAZINES, REPORTS

Manuel BAUER, 'Du Tibet à Dharamsala', *GEO magazine* (November 1995).

Kevin GARRATT, 'Tibetan Refugees, Asylum Seekers, Returnees and the Refugees Convention-Predicaments, Problems and Prospects', *Tibet Journal* 22:3 (Autumn 1997), pp. 18-56.

Timothy H. HOLTZ, 'Refugee Trauma Versus Torture Trauma: a Retrospective Controlled Cohort Study of Tibetan Refugees', *Journal of Nervous Mental Disease* 186:1 (January 1998), pp. 24-34.

International Committee of Lawyers for Tibet, *A Generation in Peril. The Lives of Tibetan Children under Chinese Rule* (Berkeley, Cal., 2001).

ICT, *Alternative Report for the Committee on the Rights of the Child. Violations of the Convention on the Rights of the Child in Tibetan Autonomous Areas of China. Country: China* (2005).

ICT, *Dangerous Crossing: Conditions Impacting the Flight of Tibetan Refugees in 2001* (2002).

ICT, *Dangerous Crossing: Conditions Impacting the Flight of Tibetan Refugees. 2002 Update* (2003).

ICT, *Dangerous Crossing: Conditions Impacting the Flight of Tibetan Refugees. 2003 Update* (2004).

ICT, *Dangerous Crossing: Conditions Impacting the Flight of Tibetan Refugees. 2004 Update* (2005).

Edward J. MILLS et al., 'Prevalence of Mental Disorders and Torture among Tibetan Refugees: A Systematic Review', *BMC International Health and Human Rights* 5:7 (2005). Published online: <http://www.biomedcentral.com/1472-698X/5/7>.

D. SERVAN SCHREIBER, B. Le Lin, B. Birmaher, 'Prevalence of Posttraumatic Stress Disorder and Major Depressive Disorder in Tibetan Refugee Children', *Journal of the American Academy of Child & Adolescent Psychiatry* 37:8 (August 1998), pp. 874-879.

TCHRD, *Education in Tibet: A briefing paper for the Special Rapporteur* (May 2003).

TCHRD, *State of Education in Tibet. A human rights perspective* (Dharamsala, 2004).

TCHRD, *Human Rights Update*, issues 1996 to 2006.

TCHRD, *Annual Report. Human Rights Situation in Tibet,* issues 2001 to 2005.

M. A. TERHEGGEN, M. S. STROEBE, R. J. KLEBER, 'Western Conceptualizations and Eastern Experience: a Cross-cultural Study of Traumatic Stress Reactions among Tibetan Refugees in India', *Journal of Trauma Stress* 14:2 (2001), pp. 391-403.

UNHCR, *Refugee Children. Guidelines on Protection and Care* (Geneva 1994).

WEBSITES

International Campaign for Tibet <http://www.savetibet.org /> This site provides an exhaustive list of Tibet linked sites under News and Information: Links.

Tibetan Centre for Human Rights & Democracy <http://www.tchrd.org/>.

TibetInfoNet <http://www.tibetinfonet.net>.

Tibet Justice Center <http://www.tibetjustice.org>.

UNHCR <http://www.unhcr.org/>.

Tibet Online <http://www.tibet.org/>.

Free Tibet Campaign <http://www.freetibet.org/>.

Students for a Free Tibet <http://www.studentsforafreetibet.org/>.

The Government of Tibet in Exile <http://www.tibet.net/>.

The official website of the Central Tibetan Administration <http://www.tibet.com/>.

Former Tibetan political prisoners association <http://www.guchusum.org/>.

DOCUMENTARY FILMS

An extensive list of films and videos about Tibet can be found at <http://www.tibet.com/>. This list includes two documentaries about child refugees:

Tibet in Exile (USA, 1991). This half-hour documentary follows the dramatic story of ten children who were smuggled out of Tibet to India. The documentary includes interviews with leaders of the community in exile, including Ms. Jetsun Pema, Director of Tibetan Children's Village and sister of His Holiness the Dalai Lama.

Escape from Tibet (UK, 1995). This documentary is about a group of young Tibetans escaping from Tibet into India. Small wonder that more and more Tibetans are escaping from the torture, persecution and oppression which they face daily in their own country. To do so they must travel 1,600 miles with no maps or specialist clothing. The journey takes them from sub-zero temperatures at an altitude of 19,000 feet through the searing heat of Kathmandu. And the elements are not their only enemy.

Three other films are:

Seeds of Tibet. Voices of Children in Exile (USA, 1997). Interviews with refugee children who have arrived in the Tibetan Homes Foundation (THF) in Mussoorie.

Flücht über den Himalaya. Kinder aud dem Weg ins Exil (Germany, 2000). This half-hour documentary follows the flight across the Himalayas of six children aged between 6 and 11. The film crew met with a group of 13 Tibetan refugees at a border pass almost 6,000 metres above sea level. They followed their escape up to their arrival in Dharamsala, northern India, where they were welcomed by the Dalai Lama. This film was granted numerous national and international awards. (The DVD includes a German and an English version). <http://www.flucht-ueber-den-himalaya.de/>.

Tibetan Refugee (USA, 2004). Stories of refugees who recount the torture and abuse they faced in Tibet and their flight out of Tibet. <http://www.vanguardcinema.com/>.